I0130182

WOMEN

STEREOTYPES AND ARCHETYPES

MANISHA ROY

© 2019 by Chiron Publications. All rights reserved. No part of this publication may be reproduced, stored in a retrieval system, or transmitted, in any form by any means, electronic, mechanical, photocopying, recording, or otherwise, without the prior written permission of the publisher, Chiron Publications, P.O. Box 19690, Asheville, N.C. 28815-1690.

www.ChironPublications.com

Interior and cover design by Cornelia G. Murariu
Printed primarily in the United States of America.

ISBN 978-1-63051-674-1 (paperback)
ISBN 978-1-63051-675-8 (hardcover)
ISBN 978-1-63051-676-5 (electronic)
ISBN 978-1-63051-677-2 (limited edition paperback)

Library of Congress Cataloging-in-Publication Data

Names: Roy, Manisha, 1936- author.
Title: Women, stereotypes and archetypes / by Manisha Roy.
Description: Ashville : Chiron Publications, [2019] | Includes
    bibliographical references and index.
Identifiers: LCCN 2018059630| ISBN 9781630516741 (pbk. : alk. paper) | ISBN
    9781630516758 (hardcover : alk. paper)
Subjects: LCSH: Women--Identity. | Women--Psychology. | Stereotypes (Social
    psychology)
Classification: LCC HQ1206 .R69 2019 | DDC 155.3/33--dc23
LC record available at https://lccn.loc.gov/2018059630

CONTENTS

PART TWO

FOREWORD

The first draft of this book was written on a typewriter nearly three decades ago and sat in one of my drawers all these years awaiting further revisions at a convenient time. If the chief editor of Chiron Publishing hadn't encouraged me to update it for publication this book may never have seen the light. The timing could not be better. I am eternally grateful to Dr. Leonard Cruz for his faith in this book and to Jennifer Fitzgerald of Chiron Publications for helping me to rework the manuscript for publication.

More than ever before modern women need to own their autonomy, dignity and sovereignty by claiming their physical, emotional, intellectual and spiritual identities. Women in America have lived through more than half a century when the Women's Liberation and the Feminist Movements succeeded in creating important economic and political benefits. Yet many women still suffer from discontent and low self-esteem resulting in loneliness, indignity and unhappiness. This is reflected in various psychosomatic illnesses, addictions and depression. I explore these conditions using cultural and psychological factors – both conscious and unconscious. Let's take one example to illustrate this point.

At the time of this book going to press, a huge number of disclosures of sexual harassments against mostly women by high profile men were followed by a spontaneous 'Me Too' movement of protest and protection of victims. In their efforts to capture the sensationalism the mainstream media lost sight of the intricacies of underlying psychology of both sides. It's more than high time to name Puritanism and promiscuity in the patriarchal social structure of this country as an opposed pair that set the arena for this game of power and lust to take place. Both the perpetrator and the victim seem to act out of confusion between what they want and what they need emotionally.

While this book does not deal with this particular issue directly, it looks at the cultural and psychological factors that taught women to accept denigration, insult and abuse from someone in a controlling position - be that a boss, a husband, a colleague or a family member. When a woman is confused about not stopping her attacker in a workplace, there is a definite disconnect between her ego and her sexuality.

I hope this book will answer some of the tangles of conundrums such as why women remain silent when they are treated with the utmost disrespect and insult. Until and unless women in America own their own identity founded on authenticity and pride and feel good being women, they will continue to collude with the patriarchal male power play unconsciously.

Manisha Roy

CAMBRIDGE

INTRODUCTION

The goal of this book is to explore the complexity of modern woman's identity, which is no longer supported by convenient but limiting stereotypic roles. In a continuously changing time and culture when the stereotypes are rejected, where in society can the majority of women find guidelines to a secure identity? How do we handle the confusion arising from such a loss? When we try to understand the confusions and answer to the questions like the following are we missing a whole dimension that is hidden, i.e., the unconscious?

- Why is it so difficult for a woman to choose between love and work? Is this dilemma a thing of the past or still daunting?

- Why does being feminine seem to mean being powerless?

- Why close relationships with men often seem unable to give space for individual development?

- Why are both women and men in traditional marriages often angry?

- Is feminism still a useful way of thinking? Are the main tenets of feminism changing?

- Is an American woman's problem of identity different than that of a woman of another culture?

In an attempt to offer answers to these key questions, I hope to resolve some of the confusion a woman in today's America and even around the globe may experience.

First of all, what is a modern woman's identity? As a sexual being, she finds herself mirrored, challenged, opposed, complemented, and sometimes abused by the other sex, man, or the society dominated by men. As a member of a society, she inherits a set of given roles, some of which nurture her as she performs them well and others she may not like. She is compelled to perform them nonetheless, and these give her problems. Personality - the expression of one's identity - thus develops and matures as the result of physical development as well as an adaptation to her cultural environment.

There is, however, a component above and beyond all this. A woman may find herself moved and led by deeper needs and desires which, in their extremes, appear to defy all other considerations and act autonomously. There may be little choice but to live them out even at the cost of losing her security; or, she may use this seemingly conflicting energy to find creative solutions. At other times, these deeper needs remain dormant or coincide with her outer life, creating fewer problems. Whichever way they are expressed, her unconscious needs constitute a vital foundation of her identity. Only if her culture and society support their expressions through prescribed roles does she become a total woman, feeling good and secure about being a woman.

Since our social system is designed to respond to the needs of the (political) majority, the minority, the weaker voice, may be heard to say that women may suffer from the conflict between inner needs and outer restrictions to express themselves. When this group increases in number, however, a change in the social structure becomes inevitable. Recently, women all over the world and in the West in particular, have experienced strong conflicts. The women's movement for nearly a century in its many variations reflected this struggle that is as much a struggle for economic, political, and social equality as a quest for identity. Is it not, to some extent then, a struggle between a woman's very (inner) identity and her (outer) roles?

A woman today expects - and, to a large extent, is expected - to be equal to men, but she needs to own and express her femininity at the same time. Because our changing society does not offer any clear-cut definitions of either femininity or masculinity, most women are confused by the increasing number of overlapping sex roles, regardless of the social or economic advantages involved. After the initial glory of success in a man's world has worn off, many modern women face severe emotional dissatisfaction. They become prime candidates for psychosomatic illnesses, addiction, or the pervasive neurosis of meaninglessness.

In general, a monumental ignorance prevails about what the real problem may be. Volumes of literature, published by social scientists, psychologists, and feminist scholars describe the social and psychological plight of modern women. During the last fifty years, most universities introduced women's studies programs, devoting time, money, and talents to the research of the historical, socio-economic, and political factors that created the present situation. Most studies offer a well-argued and well-documented diagnosis of the malady of modern women, and all of them point to the discriminating social systems run by patriarchal dominance. They point to the conclusion that if only today's women could regain the power they lost, the problems would be solved.

Only a few publications began to delve deeper into the problem. They concentrated on the emotional reality of the women themselves and addressed the puzzling and complex issue of contradictions often between emotional and outer realities. Two such examples are Susie Orbach's *Fat is a Feminist Issue* (1991), *Towards Emotional Literacy* (2001) and Luise Eichenbaum's *What Do Women Want?* (1983) and Megan Marshall's *Cost of Loving* (1984), published in England and the U.S., respectively. The women we encounter in these books are primarily victims of emotional dissatisfaction and confusion not necessarily generated by social discrimination. They confess how deeply betrayed they feel, not only by men and society, but also by their mothers, by other women, and by life itself.

Their needs for love and dependence remain unfulfilled, and they grow up to remain emotionally frustrated women who masquerade as independent and responsible adults, occupying powerful positions. Their economic independence, earned by hard work and at the expense of relationships, fails to produce emotional strength or the solidity of true identity.

Unconscious emotions that find their way into conscious behavior almost always require a readjustment of the individual's self-image. Very little is known or written about them, except in confidential case reports of psychiatric files and creative fiction and movie scripts. The number of counseling and therapy centers in American society makes the increasing need for help with this conflict more than evident. Intelligent individuals know that their destructive emotions or addictive compulsions are too powerful to be controlled by reasoning or good intentions. They also know that something is terribly wrong somewhere when people cannot even live certain parts of themselves without being branded as neurotics needing help. Yet, sometimes committing a crime or just indulging in negative emotions may make a person feel good and deeply satisfied!

We seem to lack the psychological tools to tackle such puzzles. Most analysis of social problems avoid contradictions by bypassing the emotional aspect altogether. Even though Sigmund Freud's concept of the unconscious gives one kind of explanation based on a rational and mechanistic approach, his psychoanalytic model is not always useful or effective. The conscious ego appears powerless in subduing unpredictable emotions that are often not only irrational but also arational. We lack understanding of the relevance of their existence in the total formation of the personality of both women and men. These emotions seem to defy rational analysis.

Some people, on the individual level, adapt to disturbing emotions through sublimation and creativity. Similar psychological mechanisms seem to be at work on the collective level. In fact, most of our civilization may very well be a product of a grand-scale psychological projection.[1] Unlived human emotions find symbolic expressions in art, literature, mythology, fantasies, and scientific innovations. But projections of disturbing and destructive emotions do not always find harmless channels: They are responsible for the increase in crime, child abuse, rape, hate, and mass violence in today's world. Like the rational side of our identity, the ego fails in individual cases. Law, order, and legal punishment often fail to control or rectify these problems in a social context. A rational controlling approach to very irrational problems is ultimately doomed to fail.

Therefore, along with political or economic explanations, an insight into the power of the unconscious is needed in order to understand the social malady of our time. We shy away not only from emotional factors but also tend to ignore the strong need for expressing them in some way in our lives. Our educational and social institutions are eager to introduce newer and more efficient means of legal and organizational recourse, but little is said or done regarding issues of ethical or religious values. Yet, all the time we witness the emergence of various countercultural movements, extremist religious cults, drug and narcotic cliques, all of which may be indirect expressions of unconscious needs for more irrational and emotional expressions.

In a similar fashion, the crisis of today's women may be regarded as the manifestation of an emotional discontent, not just dissatisfaction from purely economic and political inequality. We will have to take a closer look at the unconscious (and unknown) needs of the feminine psyche - needs that seem to go unfulfilled in living the existing roles. To do so, we need psychological tools that recognize and perhaps can explain some of the contradictions and paradoxes in human nature. With the help of these tools we may be able to detect where social systems fail to provide means for proper expression of human needs.

For many years during my work as an anthropologist, I studied and discussed cultural norms and human behavior and their problems in other societies based on assumptions and theories learned from my academic training. These theories were based on good, logical explanatory principles and sound arguments abstracted from Western thinking. Gradually, many questions began to emerge. For example, did my *scientific* observations about others have implications for their lives - or mine? Did these observations tell *their* reality at all? Could I be totally objective in what I observed, recorded, and presented to others? If not, what did that really mean?[2]

I also learned to use clever arguments to sidestep the issues dealing with objective and subjective tensions – something all anthropologists suffer from – but I noticed that these smart rationalizations did not always satisfy me. My emotional satisfaction came from encounters with people I studied, from my interactions with them and their culture because these encounters mirrored my challenges and compelled some sort of reckoning with myself. It became clear, after a while, that whatever created discontent in my professional life was also responsible for increasing alienation and discontent in my personal life.

But if I needed to use another society or another person to project my own unlived and unrecognized, or even unacceptable, unconscious needs, what would this lead to? If projections end in projections alone, then new discoveries I make about other people are without value unless they truly touch me. Eventually, I realized that I was interested only in those topics that were in some way relevant to my own problems. What I needed were conceptual tools or structuring principles to order my observations and experiences regarding others as well as myself. I needed to know, understand, and experience more than what my academic training had offered so far. At this point I came across C.G. Jung's writings and was deeply impressed by his approach to the human psyche.

Archetypes

C.G. Jung's concept of archetypes and the collective unconscious are valuable tools in understanding both individual and collective psychology. Archetypes include paradoxes and contradictions, which bring them closer to psychic reality and human experience than any other current Western approach.

As early as 1906, Jung discovered that some of the schizophrenic hallucinations of a Swiss man were similar to some mythological images that turned up in books of legends of the so-called normal people of a distant culture published a few years later.[3] These archaic images – or archetypes – form the impersonal and transpersonal layers of the psyche that Jung termed the collective unconscious. In the form of images, archetypes represent instincts that discharge energy and emotions while experienced.

8

Archetypes are to the psyche what instincts are to the body. Like instincts, archetypes stand for typical forms of behavior that are repeated again and again in human life and find expression through various social and cultural institutions.

Archetypes in themselves are pre-existing patterns – an *a priori* condition with a possibility of representation. They are recognized when experienced consciously, either in remembered dreams or in images, moods, and emotions released from conscious interactions with the outside world – often through projection in relationships and creative activity. Usually, the ego experiences archetypes through ambivalence of emotions that are of a gripping and compelling nature. The best example is the experience of "falling in love," whereby the ego is gripped by something bigger and has no choice but to succumb to it. Therefore, archetypes have autonomy that the ego has difficulty coping with unless it establishes a conscious connection to the archetypes.

This relationship between the ego and the unconscious, which is the most important goal of Jungian psychoanalysis, can be achieved when the symbolic images of the unconscious, as in dreams and fantasies, are allowed to participate in conscious processes, along with an emotional understanding of outer projections. Once established, this relationship helps the ego to gather newer energy and different perspectives, expanding its capacity for adaptation to both outer and inner realities. The ego, then, secures a position in the middle between the conscious, rational, outer world of our creation and the unconscious, irrational, inner world unknown to us. Thus, the ego no longer needs to gather its identity from the one-sided outer experience alone.

Archetypal experience also is characterized by a polarity of emotion, positive and negative. Mothering, for example, one of the most powerful archetypes, encompasses instincts that are loving, nurturing, and protective as well as smothering, devouring, and killing. Archetypes as such are amoral, until we experience them consciously in their paradoxical and polarized nature. These contradictions are caused by rational thinking and ethical consciousness. For example, in the process of conscious adaptation, if one pole is emphasized, the other is either repressed or projected outward. In cultures where the good mother constitutes the social ideal, the bad mother-in-law becomes a customary occurrence. Since most societies allow only partial expression of the negative pole of the archetypal patterning, most of us struggle to find a balance between the two poles. Social institutions, cultural norms, and ethical judgments of any society must reckon with this archetypal need for balance. Otherwise, the splitting of the two poles creates alienation between the ego and the archetype, and eventually leads to the eruption of negative emotions into the consciousness. This destructive move actually serves the purpose of reestablishing a balance through suffering and even danger to the well-being of the individual as well as the collective.

Compensation, as a significant recourse, is therefore closely related to the archetypal experience. Whenever there is a gross imbalance between the archetypal poles, we feel compelled to swing back to the opposite behavioral pattern, be it constructive or destructive to life. Every mother is also a daughter, every son a father, every woman a man: in other words, every role includes its opposite, and sometimes one needs to live both. An institution such as marriage, which stands for union, must also contain its opposite, i.e., separation. Otherwise, marriages break in permanent separations as the increasing statistics of divorce testifies.

The archetypal need to live one's opposite, to compensate for imbalance, is a vital point to remember when we discuss social and psychological problems. The continuous effort toward balance, either by living of the opposite or through unconscious compensation, seems to be a basic tendency of nature. Human beings are better off if they understand and participate in this process consciously. Conscious understanding also helps not to live in projections most of one's life because projections - though a natural process of life - if prolonged rob the creative energy and obstruct the paths of transformation. This happens because projections take place unconsciously and without ego's participation which is conscious, no transformation is possible. In addition, to proceed unconsciously courts a life moved by unconscious forces that often takes fateful turns. In *Memories, Dreams, Reflections* Jung wrote, "Whatever is not conscious will be experienced as fate." (Jung, 1961). The good news is that the environment, the society, and the culture support us in the struggle for balance between the conflicting inner and outer worlds.

Another aspect of the archetype is that it manifests itself in its *a priori* transpersonal quality, which transcends relationships beyond the actual experience as it takes place in an individual's lifetime. Behind the actual reality of a specific mother-daughter relationship, for example, we find a background of instinctual patterns carrying strong emotions and images. While they transcend the personal relationship, they also intensify and deepen its meaning for the individuals involved. It is not surprising, then, that age-old carriers of archetypal projections take the form of divine figures evoking strong emotions of awe and devotion as well as of fear. For a woman, this means that a significant part of her identity is rooted in the archetype of the transpersonal Mother who permeates through Mother Nature, the essence of the maternal instinct in both its constructive and destructive manifestations. The relationship between mother and daughter or father and son can, therefore, never be just personal.

Next to the parent-child relationship, the most powerful human experience is what Jung called a contrasexual experience, based on two complex archetypes termed anima and animus. Anima personifies the female principle, represented by the feminine images within a man's psyche as well as by the collective idea of femininity of his culture at the time. Conversely, animus constitutes the masculine images within a woman's psyche and the collective ideas of masculinity for a period of time in a given society and culture. Anima and animus are experienced mostly through projections, through relationships with siblings and parents, and with lovers, married partners, friends and colleagues, etc. - all of opposite sex. Since every child is born of parents of two sexes, and is usually brought up by both, the masculine and feminine archetypes vitally influence the psychic development of a woman or a man. Even ideas, principles, and institutions can carry projections of both archetypes. For a German, his country is the fatherland, whereas India is the mother to all Indians.

On many other levels, the male-female opposition in experiences and meanings of objects finds expression through sexual symbols, metaphors, and categories. Beginning with natural phenomena and ending with language, societies seem to order things according to opposite categories, often symbolized by male and female characteristics. While sky refers to vastness and spirit, which we connect with male attributes, earth and ocean are often associated with the female attributes like container, protector and nurturer. In many languages, proper and common nouns are either of masculine or feminine gender, with a few belonging to the neuter gender to specify a category that is neither. In addition, the two principles of masculine and feminine take specific connotations in a particular culture and its thought processes, and these connotations also change over time. The basic categories of opposition, however, remain, since they are based on contrasexual archetypes, eternally seeking fulfillment in the union of the opposites.

A woman's need to be united with her opposite, man, is grounded in her biosexual, psychosocial, cultural, and transpersonal archetypes. From this tension originates not only the future generation, but also creativity of all kinds. On the personal level, a woman needs to relate to her animus (whether projected on outer men or not) because her creativity and identity depend on her ego's conscious relationship to the unconscious opposite, the animus, a source of permanent tension, something that is at the root of all creativity that heals. To give a simple example, this process can be observed in a conscious, fulfilling yet struggling marriage where the wife learns more about herself by her husband's reactions. Eventually some of the projections are withdrawn when she engages herself in some creative activity and feels a sense of independence and a more satisfying sense of being. At the same time the marriage continues by transcending to another level where old mutual dependence is shifted to be followed by new ones. She gains a new perspective regarding her connection to herself – her hitherto unknown opposite side, her animus. [4]

The nature of a woman's animus is often opposed to her conscious personality, the adaptive ego, which is strongly influenced by her cultural and social environment. Ideally, her ego should be rooted in the feminine archetypes and maintain a workable relationship with her animus; the latter being realized through marriage or intimate relationship to the opposite sex and relationships with the masculine world. If her marriage is in trouble, her inner marriage with her animus is also in trouble, and vice versa. We can regard the ever-increasing divorce statistics in the modern Western world as a reflection of serious maladjustments between women and their animus, and men and their anima. I will examine this phenomenon in depth later in this book.

The function of the animus or anima is to keep the conscious ego connected to the archetypes, so that the ego is not cut off from its deeper source of the Self, the center of the collective unconscious. To maintain this balance is hard unless a woman is rooted in her cultural habits of archetypal connections via instinctive roles or various rituals, religious being one, because all religions include the transpersonal aspect through transcendence. Many modern women, who are alienated from such cultural avenues, may not have a choice but to undertake a conscious process of suffering, as in psychoanalysis. Often, however, the need to undertake an analytical process only arises after the balance has been tilted dangerously to one side or the other, as in the following example.

A 30-year-old Swiss woman started analysis because of a strong sense of being lost. She looked and dressed like a slightly robotic androgynous being and gave me the impression of being somewhere else or nowhere in particular. She was physically attractive, educated, and held an adequate job. She also had occasional boyfriends. As an only child, she felt quite close to her parents. All these facts did not help her to build a secure self-image. She seemed to be in a state of mild-grade depression all the time despite being somewhat functional with adequate insights about her problems.

It took nearly four years of analysis - which often bored both of us - before she began to show signs of emotional reaction. The impact of her rich dream and fantasy life started to affect her emotionally, and she began to create some artistic work on her own. She built little boxes - 6 to 7 inches wide, high and deep with open fronts showing things inside. She used fabric or colored papers to decorate the interior of the boxes and put handmade miniature objects and figurines inside each one, creating a story. One such box told me that she was on drugs when she was a teenager. Her dreams also began to show recurrence of certain feminine figures, the impact of which she could not shake off and remained mostly inattentive like an earlier time in analysis. Around this time, she also changed her job to an all-women organization. Now, every day became a struggle with her women co-workers, and after one year she left for a week to go to a retreat, just to get away. While there, she had the worst nightmare, threatening her severely. She became physically ill and was in total despair. As she sobbed in her bed alone one night, she had a vision: A veiled feminine figure enveloped her and held her in her arms, comforting her. She felt better immediately and could go back to sleep.

A week after this incident, she terminated analysis, stating that she no longer needed me, that she felt stronger and as if a mysterious link had been established with something bigger than herself. When she told me about her vision, I was deeply moved and had a numinous experience of the veiled figure myself. My patient's unconscious had chosen a critical breaking point in her life to evoke the archetypal image of the feminine and protective principle. Now rooted in her archetype, she began to regain her lost identity as a woman.

As a Swiss woman born and brought up in a cultural environment whose values are based on technological progress and strong Protestant work ethics, she did not find her natural femininity supported and reinforced either by her mother or by her society. Cultures that still value femininity both in outer nature and in people's mentality seem to have reduced problems in this regard. Sensitive travelers always remark that despite abject poverty how secure women of Third World countries like Africa and India appear to be.

Since the analytical process is concerned mainly with the unconscious, it is hard to define in rational terms in such a brief example what exactly brought about the gradual blossoming of self-realization and sense of a secure identity for this woman. Many factors come together in the painful process of years of analysis. In this case, part of the work was done through the unconscious relationship and identification with the woman analyst, part through the patient's dreams and fantasies and her own creative efforts as well as honest search in finding her lost self.

Obviously, concepts such as archetypes are more readily available to people who have had the experience of Jungian psychoanalysis. These concepts, however, can be accessible to everybody if they are explained in the context of experiences that we all share, at one point or another, in our lives. The introduction of psychological terms into everyday language requires awareness among ordinary people regarding the unconscious and its significance. Terms such as *complex, unconscious, ego, projection,* and many others have already become parts of our everyday vocabulary though not always used correctly. Freud could not have been as successful if people had not been ready for his insights regarding the significance of the unconscious over a century ago. The need to find and use more comprehensive and flexible concepts, such as the archetypes, is overdue and must not be restricted to Jungian scholars alone.

The Cultural Component

Although I was born and brought up in India, as a young woman, I moved to the West and was educated, worked, married, and lived most of my life in America and Western Europe. As a result, my own identity has been put to serious tests. My professional training as an anthropologist studying many different cultures, and, later, as a Jungian psychoanalyst working with people from outside my own culture, added further to the complexities I experienced. I came to realize that I needed to understand my own and others' identity problems, both comparatively and within the context of one's own culture and society.

Today, in a world that seems to be smaller and more complex daily, a woman's life is a composite of many roles, many exciting choices, and much confusion. I found the archetypes to be a helpful tool in sorting out these confusions and tensions. Archetypes explain human actions and behavior on an experiential level, so that we arrive at a deeper understanding of the foundations of what connects various contexts and different identities across cultures. Knowing the archetypal background of one's culture and upbringing helps the ego to recognize and acknowledge the solidity of one's identity that transcends all fragmented identities lived in various roles.

My personal need to find a meaningful connection between the many worlds I lived in also made me aware of the relativity of an individual's experiences within the framework of a specific culture. An educated woman in India, for example, can hold a profession and feel comfortable with all her family roles at the same time, whereas her Western counterpart most likely experiences some conflict. Social and cultural differences make an American woman view her salaried job not only as an economic advantage but as a definite enhancement of her self-image as well. If her family roles are in conflict with her job, they are in conflict with her identity too.

While all women share the same basic archetypal needs and emotions, how they recognize and cope with these needs depends a great deal on the individual's cultural and social endowments and values. A woman's identity is the product of her innate nature as it has been shaped, reinforced, or opposed by her cultural environment. The influence of these cultural norms and social rules persists in varying degrees throughout her life. Childhood and old age are relatively free of restrictions, while adolescence and the adult to middle years are particularly influenced by group values. Peers and neighbors may determine much of a woman's ethical standards and choices, and her identity consists to a large extent of what her immediate culture and social environment define as a "good woman."

How cultural images of femininity may vary over time within the same society is exemplified well by the changing concept of the American woman during the last 70 years. What was outrageous and exceptional 50 years ago is commonplace today. Yet, we also find a tendency in nearly every decade or so to reverse the previous pattern, as if to compensate for the extremes of the former time.

During the Seventies, the daughters of dependent housewives rejected their mothers' role model and became independent professionals. In the Eighties, they were searching for emotional and material security again. Some were ready to sacrifice their economic independence for some sort of emotional commitment, within or without marriage. This state of affair continued through the Nineties with more and more women becoming relaxed about proving themselves in the workplace and marketplace. The practice of conventional marriage and motherhood returned and took hold of many women with a force, and they not only chose motherhood over professions, some of them became "tiger" and "helicopter" mothers, carrying the projection of the extremes as a compensation of the previous generation. However, changes in the definition of a woman's roles vary at different levels of economic sections, in different age groups, and even in different stages of a woman's life.

Stereotypes

Social institutions and customs are necessary and essential parameters for the realization of archetypes in an individual's life. This ongoing experience also forms the identity of a person. Roles offer channels through which we may not only express our instinctive needs, but also live indirectly those emotions that are negative. Family roles, based on heritage and deep unconscious connections, are the most important because they carry so many of our projections. Our greatest satisfactions and worst disappointments come out of relationships with our family members. Nowhere do we live more intensely than within our families. Women of all societies and of all generations must fulfill the stereotypes of being daughters, sisters, wives, mothers, grandmothers, and many more roles.

Stereotypes emerge over time, from role-behavior models, when roles become typical and habitual and allow us to eliminate conflicts as much as possible. For the majority, it is easier to fall into stereotypes because they create fewer tensions, although some may need the excitement that comes from breaking the rules. These pioneers who rebel against stereotypes may fall into a new set of stereotypes. What is unconventional today becomes conventional tomorrow. Younger people break away from the stereotypes their parents live, only to find themselves living their own. Whether followed or rejected, stereotypes remain the guidelines of behavior and the basis for security and identity because stereotypes help us to know what is expected of us in any given situation.

Roles that are stereotypes are social expressions of archetypes, but they often become the outer frame only and are somewhat disconnected from the archetypal and emotional roots. Thus, when the role stereotypes are broken and the actors are confused, over time newer expressions and forms of the archetypes emerge. Without the roles becoming stereotypes, however, one does not try to break them. Stereotypes that become hackneyed and meaningless are the essential first steps for archetypes to become revitalized. Women and men who reject stereotypes as role models opt for a confused phase of their identity. Only a few have enough strength to go through this. For the majority, living in stereotypes is the only means of obtaining at least a certain amount of security. Some individuals even gain their totality and integrity by assuming their stereotypic roles naturally.

In modern times, fewer and fewer roles allow a balanced expression of instinctual needs. In most advanced societies, the basic needs of food, shelter, mating, and mothering are satisfied in terms of individual's rational decisions. We are encouraged to make conscious choices instead of following a dictated set of rules, as previous generations did. Yet, our basic and most primary identity derives from satisfying instinctive and unconscious roles. Fluidity of role structure, therefore, confuses most people. Even the pioneers who break free from the restrictions of defined roles revert to their own set of stereotypes, because they, too, need the security of the group's approval and support. Stereotypes, then, can be regarded to be the essential social boundaries of our collective identity up to a point.

Throughout history, women in most societies have been the custodians of culture and customs, whether in an Indian village, where women are responsible for the continuity of household religious rituals, or in a Western city, where mostly women serve in the various organizations connected to social services and the arts. Until recently women have been encouraged to pursue roles that correspond naturally with their family roles. If suddenly women are confused as to what is expected of them, a change is signaled. They need to break out of the old stereotypes, which have become unsatisfying and no longer contribute toward a renewed identity. To do so, however, they also need a conscious understanding of what constitutes their present identities, and which cultural and social influences are at work.

The knowledge and awareness of the significance of archetypes in her life may help a woman to sort out conflicts, since with it comes an awareness of herself as it is rooted in the unconscious. She can regain a sense of belonging to something that is bigger than life by experiencing the various, and often contradictory aspects of her emotions instead of just following unexamined *images* and *ideas*. Archetypes will help her to accept many kinds of emotions in herself and in others, whether they are positive and desirable - such as love and caring - or negative feelings of hate, power, and frustration. The rejection of stereotypic roles by today's woman is virtually a search for newer roles that allow the expression of paradoxes and contradictions. The true identity of a woman who feels good about herself can be achieved only through the realization that comes from experiencing a combination of archetypal needs and stereotypic roles, which in turn are enriched by the archetypal connection made consciously.

The first part of this book discusses the cultural variations and expressions of archetypal experience; in the second part, I attempt to show the emotional impact of archetypes on individual lives of modern American women and how each individual woman recognizes and copes with her identity problem in a unique way. In the conclusion, some of the theoretical issues are summarized, including the transpersonal and transcendental aspects of archetypes as they exist beyond specific societies and cultures. If the purpose of all knowledge is not only to understand how things work, but also to find meaning that enriches our lives and heals our souls, an archetypal approach to human behavior certainly brings us closer to that end.

One last point needs mentioning. I urge the reader to keep an open mind and take an intuitive approach to this complex topic. Understanding of the archetypal aspects of one's personality must come from both heart and mind. My arguments are not only based on logical and sociological facts, but on mythology and psychology as well, as I perceive the topic through intuitive insights and emotional experience. The validity of these observations must come from a shared experience between the author and the reader, illuminated, I hope, by occasional sparks of insight and familiarity. The credibility of my observations and conclusions cannot depend on terse logic of scientific proof alone.

ENDNOTES

1 See Marie-Louise von Franz's (1985) *Projection and Re-Collection in Jungian Psychology: Reflections of the Soul*, La Salle, Illinois: Open Court.

2 Manisha Roy's book *The Reckoning Heart: An Anthropologist Looks at her Worlds* (2001) was born out of this dilemma in the field.

3 Jung, C.G (1956) Symbols of Transformation, *Collected Works*, vol 5, paragraph 151-154 and 222-225.

4 See Manisha Roy (1990) "Developing the Animus as a Step Toward the New Feminine Consciousness" In *To Be A Woman* (Ed) Connie Zweig, Los Angeles: Jeremy P. Tarcher Inc. pp. 137-149.

PART ONE

CHAPTER 1

Cultural
Archetypes

Introduction

The two chapters in Part 1 attempt to show how archetypal experiences are relative to the cultural environment and that specific histories, social systems, and religious beliefs and practices give rise to something I like to call cultural archetypes.[5] Cultural archetypes simply mean that while all humans share the same archetypal drives and emotions, the images and behaviors expressing them vary enough from culture to culture, producing symbols and experiences peculiar to each culture in space and time. Moreover, manifestations of the archetypes seem to evolve within the context of a society's history and tradition shaping its people's life and destiny.

To demonstrate the workings of the cultural aspect of the archetype, I shall look first at the historical, social, and psychological environment of a Western woman's life, drawing from my years of experience as an anthropologist and psychotherapist. Here, too, I shall use C.G. Jung's concepts as tools to understand a woman's psychology within a given time and space.

The second chapter follows with a discussion of the mythology, psychology, and sociology of Hindu India, where I was born and brought up until early youth. We will see the differences in the two cultural experiences as they are reflected in both the archetypal and the external behavior.[6]

Western Experience: Setting the Stage

Western women who enter psychoanalysis often do so because they suffer from the intense conflict between dreams of what they want and what life offers them. The discrepancy between what a woman should do or be and what she wishes to be is an age-old problem. In recent decades, however, such conflicts seem to be exacerbated by the gap between social and cultural ideals and a woman's instinctive and archetypal needs. The crucial question that remains is why despite many outward successes and choices, many women are still not content with life. Why are women often disillusioned about their achievements and confused as to who they are and what they really want?

For most women, this pain comes from not having control over their emotional lives. Sheer determination seems to fail to make them comfortable with themselves and others. "Why doesn't the economic success help in dealing with this sense of meaningless existence?" they ask. Looking for the reasons of their emotional problems in the past and in family history cannot satisfy them either.

When the blames are based on some sort of psychological understanding, it helps somewhat. But they continue to repeat the same destructive patterns of addiction or other harmful habits. For others, even the problem itself is not clear; only a vague and persistent feeling of frustration envelops their whole existence. Nothing seems to be exciting or enriching. Life is a routine and a drag.

Then, there is a large group of women who suffer from psychosomatic ailments that do not get better even after years of medical treatment. Symptoms shift around and manifest in different parts of the body. Many of them join groups and programs to deal with their bulimia, addiction, obsession, and dysfunction. Others resign and take over-the counter pills and watch talk shows on national television and feel somewhat consoled that they are not the only ones.

These disillusionments, whether emotionally felt or masked in physical pain, render women of different ages and backgrounds unhappy and helpless. The worst pain, however, comes from the realization that the situation is uncontrollable by the ego's will and power.

Perhaps the problem and its solution lie not in the realm of the ego as much as somewhere deeper inside ourselves — in the deep core of our psyche. Our emotional life seems out of control because ego is not supported by the deeper Self—an essential combination for the self-sufficiency and wholeness in a human being. Only then can a woman (or a man) tolerate and live with the existential suffering and be free of painful neurotic symptoms, because the symptoms appear in the first place to attract ego's attention to the soul.

This book, therefore, is also about how to help the ego listen to these symptoms and make the connection to the soul — a healing process, not just curing the symptoms.

In the medieval Celtic myth of the King Arthur's adventures, the wise old hag claimed that a woman, more than anything, wanted sovereignty over her own life. (See renderings of the Wife of Bath's Tale, or The Marriage of Sir Gawain.) Eight centuries later, this self-sovereignty still remains the true quest in a modern woman, whether she is conscious of it or not.

Unfortunately, the majority of our lives show that either we have forgotten the quest or are ignorant of the way to go about it. Is it because we have lost the wise witch who knows the real purpose of a woman's life, although many women seem to have quite a bit of Arthur inside them? Today's woman has shown bravery and competence in life's adventures no less than the Celtic king himself.

In the Grail legend of King Arthur and the Round Table (see Sir Gawain and the Green Knight), there is a tale that is appropriate for our discussion. King Arthur, who trespassed on a local king's property to poach in his river, was about to lose his Round Table to the king unless he could answer the question, "What do women really want?" Arthur had one year to find the answer. When only one day was left and he still did not know the answer, he was desperate. He was advised by the Knights of the Round Table to go and solicit help from the old witch at the edge of the forests who was shunned by all for her ugliness but was recognized for her wisdom. The old witch said she would give Arthur the right answer provided Arthur promised to offer his noblest Knight, Gawain, in marriage to her! Arthur was stunned by this unreasonable price but had no choice but to agree to this horrible bargain. The answer to the question of what does a woman really want was: "She wants sovereignty over her own life."

To save Arthur's honor and the Round Table, the loyal knight Gawain agreed to marry the ugly witch, who, of course, turned out to be the bewitched princess when he accepted the witch with respect and honor. But Gawain could have his beautiful bride only during the day or at night, and she asked him to choose one. Wise Gawain, however, let the lady make the decision herself and was rewarded for his surrender to the wisdom and sovereignty of the feminine. He won the beautiful bride for both day and night!

This little tale from the Grail myth and many others like it around the world hold clues to the solution to the unhappiness of both women and men of our time. The ugly hag changes into a beautiful princess only when the noble knight accepts her with respect, dignity, and surrender. To read this surrender literally as domination of man by the woman would be a serious blunder.

This myth demonstrates beautifully how ancient feminine wisdom can transform itself, at least through the humble recognition from the hero. Does a modern woman, then, need to surrender her heroic side to the long-forgotten old witch within herself? I really believe that it is the only way she can find herself and have her own sovereignty.

Before she can do that, she first needs to recognize and understand the exact nature of her problem. She needs to know the hero within and how to use him. Only an Arthurian ego can command a Gawain to face the old witch, the negative but potentially wise feminine side. A big part of our pain comes from the confusion of not knowing these potentials within us. Most of the time we are pawns to the collective stereotypes — roles we learn to play without questions, but do not always fulfill our inner needs. Thus, we are confused in our social identity as well. Lately, women in America (and gradually all over the world) have taken the heroic stand to at least question these roles.

For example, we want to be equal to men in their "privileged" positions of power, rights, and responsibilities. But we do not know how to do that without losing our femininity. Being primarily patriarchal, the culture offers little value to the feminine mode of existence. And women are as much a part of this patriarchal system as their male counterparts.

Acceptance and surrender that the Celtic knight used appropriately to appease and win the feminine wisdom and its benefit are part of the feminine mode of being. One can add other qualities such as relatedness, receptivity, endurance, and sacrifice — all so-called old-fashioned feminine traits that are hardly a part of our upbringing today. Most of these qualities are viewed with a negative judgment by both women and men. Either they are considered signs of weakness or used for manipulative purposes. Only the witch, not her wisdom, remains. What then has gone wrong to create this one-sided attitude?

I hope to sort out some of these tangles and suggest ways of finding the hero within who, in turn, can help us reclaim our wise femininity. This quest is a psychological adventure that is challenging and painful hard work, but ultimately rewarding.

My own experience and with other women I encounter in life and analytic practice, tells me exactly what the tale above demonstrates. It is clear that the solutions to our disillusionments and helplessness with our lives must be sought in both feminine and masculine experiences in the outer and inner worlds. For both these realms not only reflect and express one another but also need to come to a balance of a sort. It is a journey that goes forward and backward forming many circles that encompass our total lives.

Another way of putting it would be to use the metaphor of biological conception and birth. The birth of a child — beginning with the first encounter of the sperm and the egg, the fertilization, the gestation for nine months and the final expulsion of the child through the birth canal — all involve a combination of both feminine and the masculine modes. Any woman who has given birth physically knows how much she had to be patient during her pregnancy, to surrender to the nature's rhythm of the growing fetus, and yet be aggressive to push the baby out during birth. Likewise, any woman or man who has ever given birth to any creative work knows how much she or he has to be both the aggressive *male* and the patient, enduring *female* at the same time. And since I like to think that "living" itself is the most creative of all endeavors, we have to follow the same attitude to make it worth living.

More specifically, for a modern woman to deal with the pain and confusion with her life, she needs her masculine traits, i.e., her proactive, aggressive side to help her to reconnect to her lost femininity before she can be self-born again and find her sovereignty. I realize the statement above sounds like a dangerous proposition for many of us who have already suffered from the patriarchal oppression for generations. How can we accept help from the same male partners who usurped our existence and either ignored or dominated our lives and souls for centuries? How can the same brute turn into the noble knight who surrenders to our wisdom first so we can be helped by him later?

This impossible task may not be so impossible if we begin with a slightly different question. Could men violate our existence without some sort of *unconscious* collaboration on our part? It was one of the first feminists who dared to pose this most pertinent question nearly 70 years ago. In her path-breaking book *The Second Sex* (first published in 1949), Simone de Beauvoir invited us to be aware of our role, our responsibility in men's oppression of us. After more than half a century of painful struggle by women through various movements and personal lives, I do not feel that we have asked this question with full honesty yet.

The hard struggle of the feminist movement during the '60s and '70s bore fruit in the '80s onward in obtaining economic rights and professional respectability, if not full equality. Now during the early part of the 21st century, many of us are profoundly aware of the emotional price that has been paid for these changes. Many women are still deeply dissatisfied with work, love, marriage, motherhood, and other relationships. Many women feel they have not received the financial gains promised to them despite equal qualifications with their male counterpart. Others feel alienated from families, from partners, from themselves.

At the close of 1989 a *Time* magazine issue described the painful scenario and confusion of exhausted and disillusioned women of the '80s as they stepped into the decade of the '90s. After thorough research and many interviews with women from various walks of life, the reporter sadly realized that despite the sincere struggle and determination on the part of so many women and men, the outcome of the feminist movement over two decades failed to fulfill the promise of a better self-image and self-respect. One must admit, however, that some of the economic and legal goals were achieved.

For example, by 1990, more than half of America's workforce consisted of women compared with only 34 percent during 1960s. The number of professional women in law, medicine, engineering, journalism, and even the military rose to a high proportion during this period. Yet, the bitterest complaints came from women between 30 and 40 who put career before marriage and motherhood. They were faced with successful jobs and lonely lives. At the other end of the spectrum, stay-at-home mothers with children under 18 (who made up one-third of American women) were even more dissatisfied. Not only had they sacrificed professions and economic independence, but they also felt devalued by the feminist ideals that undermined their choice of motherhood over profession.

By the end of the '80s, some veteran feminists such as Betty Friedan were already suggesting that men be included in the movement. During this time, over 600 women's business organizations were born, and they were fighting for practical solutions to problems that concerned both women and men, such as better child care benefits, abortion rights, shared jobs, etc. Apparently, some men were beginning to appreciate these changes because the workplace with a female presence made it pleasant and more interesting. Cooperation was more attractive, and the general atmosphere in the workplace was not fraught with male competition. According to this report, more and more men were prepared to sacrifice part of their work time and wages to be with their families. Married men were sharing 30 percent of the housework compared with 20 percent two decades earlier.

This trend in partnership at home and at work had been supported by the latest feminists and the expressed goal of the 600-odd women's business organizations mentioned above. However, not all were happy. A reaction began to set in by the end of the '80s, especially among men. The decade of the '90s saw the rise of a men's separatist movement, which fought to reclaim men's privileges. In the privacy of the therapy rooms and among themselves, some men began to voice the anger and resentment of being used by the one-sided feminist goals. Many of them were afraid of losing whatever *masculinity* they had left. They were nervous about being too feminized, although they also saw the ideological and practical value of a fuller partnership. Several all-male organizations, groups and conferences were being organized around the country. The poet Robert Bly, archetypal psychologist James Hillman, and some others were attempting to offer a sense of male initiation experience to their followers and readers.

I encountered women and men around this time in my practice and in life who confessed their confusion and bitterness. However, there was one difference. Women who made the first step to seek out help knew that the practical solution suggested by the 600-odd business organizations was not the only issue. Some of them were ready to rebel against the self-inflicted ideal of the superwoman who must play every role and multitask to the satisfaction of an ideal they had a hard time believing anymore. They knew that their unhappiness had to do with a totally unrealistic goal they at one point believed — that this lifestyle would offer them emotional satisfaction. Many seek help, even today, to alleviate painful symptoms such as headaches, backaches, insomnia, and obsessions and addictions. These candidates for psychotherapy with myriad psychosomatic symptoms then and now know that the problems lay somewhere else and that simply outer solutions do not address the real problem. Many of these women may not lack the insights, although may lack the courage to do something about their discontent.

This alienation is exacerbated by the advent and all-pervasive influence of information technology during last few decades that allowed many younger women to compete in a man's world, efficiently earning financial success but not contentment. The conflicts between career and motherhood remained, if only delayed as a young generation of women opted to become mothers after their success in the workplace. The fast-moving cyber communication technology has brought along changes of human values and attitudes that could not be foreseen or predicted. Both women and men bit into the new apple not in the biblical Heaven but in the "silicon valleys" of the corporate worlds around the globe. The impact of this new lure is yet to be fully realized. One thing is clear: This new interloper is going to change the rules of the game for not only women and men but also their children. In her book *The Hero's Daughter* (1994), Maureen Murdock quotes a woman who worked in computer science. What this woman said in 1994 is even more appropriate today. Let me quote from the very first page of *The Hero's Daughter:* "Women who join a high-tech company enter a very masculine model where competition is fierce and the survivors are those in whom the male fighter is strong. Feelings of compassion, understanding, and support are dangerous to one's career. In my ten years of working in Silicon Valley, I have not met one woman who feels good about herself and hasn't abdicated her femininity..." [7]

That is the picture of the beginning of the new millennium's post-cyber revolution. Let me reverse gears for a bit longer to trace the progression of this and other phenomena that have given rise to the extreme dissatisfaction among at least a sizable proportion of women who had no clue as to what constituted their happiness and contentment. They went headlong to achieve everything men achieved before them.

However, there are women like Linda who followed a moderate route yet faced serious conflicts. A woman of 35 and a mother of two boys (ages 6 and 3), Linda is a part-time college professor. Her husband, also a professor in the same field, works full time and is very busy publishing to advance his tenure track. Linda willingly sacrificed the full-time position to spend more time with her children who, of course, spend part of the day at school and day care. Her complaint is that she ends up doing most of the chores in the household although her husband tries to share as much as his busy schedule permits. It is not enough. She is going all day from errand to errand like a robot, and in the evening after the boys go to bed, she must prepare for her lectures. As a young girl, she trained as a pianist as well as a modern dancer. Now she has no time or desire to do either. She feels like a machine that does her job and her duties without pleasure. She is sensitive enough to know that she must do something to change this regimen. Otherwise, she will end up a wreck, she says.

Linda's case sounds like a no-win situation. Her husband is one of those post-feminist-movement men who believes that men should share equally in housekeeping. Linda willingly sacrificed her professional ambition to be a wife/mother. She loves her husband and children. Yet her life seems to steal something important from her. As she feels dissatisfied, she also feels guilty. "Why do I feel this way? I should be fulfilled with everything I have. What's wrong with me?" Her question cannot be answered by shifting around the outer life arrangement. There is no particular change possible or even wanted by her. It's not a question of doing it differently.

Pam, age 33, who is very much in Linda's position with one child and no profession, complains about the same. Only her understanding is slightly different. She seems to think that if only she knew what she wanted, she would do it differently. She would not marry and be a mother. She would go for a career and might think of a marriage later. At least she could enjoy having more time for herself. Now she spends every single day going from one chore to the next. Even the holidays and weekends are full of logistics, organization, details. "Does it get any better when the kids leave home and we're older?" she asks. In response to Pam's question, I could tell her about Linda or someone else to show that her professional sisters are not in any better position when it comes to inner satisfaction and self-worth.

For several years I watched Susan, my neighbor, jog every morning without fail. Susan is in her late 30s, single, attractive, healthy, and slim. She works as a financial expert in a big investment firm and seems to have her life under control. She jogs every morning for an hour, goes to work, goes out with men or women after work, comes home, goes to bed to get up early next day to jog again. She is waiting for Mr. Right, who will take her off her feet, take her in his arms, and marry her. She will then work part time and have a few kids and live happily ever after.

This fantasy, she knows, is not going to work because she has women friends like Linda and Pam. But she nurtures the fantasy anyway, because that's all she has. Otherwise, life is so boring that she would not like to continue it. "I tried to take vacations in the Bahamas, date attractive guys and buy new wardrobes. I can afford all this, but I can't seem to afford happiness. That's why I have created this fantasy." It took her many more months before she admitted to me one day, that she had been drinking and taking drugs to boost up her fantasy life. This bothered her very much, considering her concerns about health. It was as if it were another woman within her who craved these destructive habits and defeated the well-meaning part of herself. Now, she was scared — scared of losing control totally.

In the '90s Linda, Pam, and Susan, all in their 30s, were facing some crises unlike many of the younger age group. By the end of the '90s, women younger than 30 already became aware about the situation and planned a different strategy. They wanted careers *and* families, and expected to have husbands who would be real partners in every sphere of their lives. They took equality for granted. They did not have to fight for it. Many of them did not like to be called feminists although they claimed to be feminine.

These expectations sound more ideal than real. But they were still young and could afford to be idealistic. They could perhaps even avoid the problems their older sisters faced. Only time would tell. Few young women of this age group come to therapy, and those were perhaps exceptions.

To move to a slightly older group for a moment, I want to talk about Cheryl who represents by far the most typical problem I encounter in my work. At 43, Cheryl is a successful physician. Her exceptional academic credentials followed by a rapidly rising career already made her a recognized medical specialist. She earns over $280,000 a year, owns a nice house, an expensive car, and has a very busy schedule. Her too-busy a schedule, she complains, allows her little time to enjoy her beautiful home, which is looked after by a well-paid gardener and a housekeeper. During the first three years of her job in a well-endowed private hospital, she felt more fortunate than most of her male colleagues.

However, this highly successful, attractive woman is puzzled by her inability to attract any interesting man. She is reaching an age and a stage of her life that is creating severe anxiety. She cannot just use excuses anymore of not having time or not needing men. "I work late every evening because I dread coming home — my beautiful home. I am terribly lonely when I am not at the hospital. Can you believe that a woman like me feels inadequate because I don't have a man in my life? I envy my cleaning woman, who goes on and on about her husband who drinks and picks violent fights with her. I feel like telling her, 'Don't complain. You don't know how lucky you are.'

"Oh yes," she continued, "I tried some personal columns and dating services. Nothing seems to work after one or two dates. I don't know what's wrong with me. Some men are scared, I suppose. I make more money than many men of my age, if not in my profession. Doctors don't like to date doctors seriously. They know that marriage with another doctor would make a family impossible unless one of them sacrifices the career. At this point, I won't mind sacrificing my career if I had a man who would love and marry me. I wish I knew how to build a relationship. More important, I wish I knew why I need a man so badly. One would think I should be content. But my success fails to sustain me. I need a personal life where I can forget the stress of my profession." Then after a long pause Cheryl asks, "What's the secret my cleaning woman has and I don't?"

Cheryl's confession touched me deeply. Despite her intelligence and overdeveloped competence, her vulnerability was disarming. What is it in her that makes her need a man so badly yet subverts her ability to do so? I had to admit that there was something missing in her. She lacked a depth and a dimension despite all her academic success and professional abilities.

Within a year into her analysis, it became evident that Cheryl needed to go deep into herself to discover who she was as a woman, not as a competent "man." She confessed her envy not only of her cleaning woman but of many others, including a woman colleague. This woman was "sexually compulsive" (as Cheryl put it) and seduced everyone available. Cheryl condemned her yet could not help being envious. In a series of dreams, the sexy colleague appeared, culminating in one where she seduced the dreamer. Cheryl woke up from this dream feeling very happy and sexually aroused. She was puzzled by this reaction but seemed to have realized something deeper within herself.

It took our successful doctor another four years of intensive analysis and therapy before she began to look and feel self-sufficient enough to make some drastic changes in her life. In the meantime, many more dreams came that portrayed sacrificed male figures, some known, some unknown. One of the dreams had an African medicine man who asked her to follow him and disappeared in the dark. This dream kept repeating in different versions for several months. Something more solid and definite seemed to be forming inside her. One day, she mentioned that she was planning to apply for an overseas job.

I never saw Cheryl so ecstatic when she announced that she got a job offer in Africa and signed a contract for five years! Before she left, she came to say goodbye. She thanked me for helping her to be on the right path to find herself. Six months later, I received a small parcel and a brief note from her. The parcel contained a lovely ebony statue of an African woman. The note said: "... I work hard to help the women to take care of their children who suffer from malnutrition even before they are born. Each time I hold a sick baby in my arms, I feel so good that I wonder how that is possible! My life is busy and full, and every evening after a long day's work I look forward to return to my modest hut, where I feel more myself than I ever felt in my Boston brownstone ..."

If Cheryl's story sounds too good to be true, it is because in a brief description it is not possible to capture all of her painful experience during the long time we worked together. I intend to return to her story later in this book. Her intelligence and her determination to help herself made her heroic enough to take the challenge. She also surrendered to her primitive sexual side, her wise witch, at least, emotionally. Cheryl was fortunate to have had the basic requirement – psychological courage to undertake the difficult journey inward. But many women lack the honesty and courage to do so.

Women who are older have other kinds of frustrations. The cliché of middle-aged married women being deserted by their husbands for younger women happens to be a common crisis they face. This marital crisis for the middle-aged couple can bring about psychological independence for both partners. More often than not, however, a woman in this kind of marriage spends a lot of time blaming, avenging, and finally being separate in a long-drawn-out divorce. Many of these bitter women end up being victims of psychosomatic illnesses or some kind of addiction. Those who can resist victimization seem to benefit from the separation despite (and perhaps because of) the traumatic emotional hardship from the betrayal, which ushers them to an emotional journey.

Sometimes, only a painful divorce may humble the bitter ego to look inside. However, women who learn to take such an experience as a mirror to look at themselves, are few. The majority remain stuck in the "victim" role, making themselves and people around them miserable. Sixty-seven year-old Margaret, however, was an exception.

Married before finishing college, Margaret followed her husband to his new job all the way to the other end of the country. Although a good student, she left her studies gladly because she wanted to marry the man she loved and could not wait to set up a household for the two of them. She loved being Mrs. So and So. It gave her a sense of identity. All this was nearly 30 years earlier. During the next 10 years, she remained busy bringing up their four children and never regretted being a mother. Her husband was not only a good provider but also an attentive partner.

"Whenever the kids had any crisis, both my husband and I sat down with them and tried to work it out. We had our shares of problems with children. But I knew that he was always by my side. I had what might be called an "ideal marriage." Margaret continued with her own story: "During the '70s, my last son went to school in England, and suddenly I had a real empty nest. I kept myself busy with my tennis group, museum auxiliary, and other social engagements we were involved in those days. It took me another three years before I began to realize another kind of emptiness. By now I was 45 years old. It all began with my oldest son bringing home his fiancée one Thanksgiving.

"She was a bright, intensely lively 20 year-old. Talking with her, I was suddenly hit by a pang of jealousy. I realized that I would never have the opportunities she had. My contentment of being a full professor's wife and mother of four great sons looked meaningless all on a sudden. I talked to my husband about it, and he solved the problem quickly by suggesting that I should go back to school and take some courses or something. Since he was a faculty member, I could go to his university free of charge.

"I took his advice and began to take a few Continuing Education courses and even enjoyed them. But somehow, I couldn't shake off the sense of hidden envy I felt of my daughter-in-law. Only if I were born 20 years later! I began to feel out of place in my own home. My previous interests in gardening, in parties, in my friends all began to pale considerably. I was scared at this point because I wasn't sure what was wrong with me. Only thing I knew was that I needed to do something else, be somewhere else, be someone else."

At this point, life itself intervened with an opportunity. Her husband was invited to be at a university in Australia for a year. She decided not to accompany him. For the first time in her long marriage, she did not follow him. It was not easy because she enjoyed traveling and exploring new countries. Her husband, as usual, supported her decision, and her sons and the daughter-in-law encouraged her strongly to follow her feelings.

During that year, she discovered a few truths about herself. A woman friend invited her to a workshop given by a Sufi spiritual man, which impressed her profoundly. She knew now that she needed a teacher to lead her to the path of a spiritual journey, and that was what was missing in her life. Once felt, the intuition soon became a decision. She found such a guide and became deeply involved in her inner work through meditation and dreams. Before I close Margaret's story, let her speak the last words for herself.

"I'm so fortunate that I bumped into my friend that day when she casually invited me to that workshop. I feel so much in tune with myself and more in peace than I could imagine possible. When my husband decided to stay on in Australia and asked for a divorce, I could say "yes." My sense of being betrayed was tolerable. I have already begun to find myself without him. I feel a bit jealous and left out sometimes, but also relieved that he, too, found his own way without me. Our marriage of 35 years was no more essential for either of us."

Margaret began to teach a class of painting and meditation to a group of women and even began to support herself. She looked very content as she said, "My artwork and my teaching take me more and more to myself. It's wonderful; it's like finding a bit of God every day." I saw a woman who really discovered the deepest center of herself at a ripe age.

Margaret is an exception than the rule. Many married women after 20 or 30 years of marriage and motherhood may not be as lucky. They find themselves in the middle of their lives without youth or peace of mind. They lack imagination or inclination to reinvent themselves. The society and culture do little to help women of this age, except reminding them of their lost youth. Without the right guidance, many are lost and lonely and do not know how to turn their loneliness into an introversion that will take them back to themselves. They have been brought up in a strongly extroverted culture where being alone is considered as being unfortunate. They have learned to avoid introversion as an abnormal behavior.

The midlife crisis hits a woman no less seriously than it hits her husband. In his case, there is a tacit understanding that he may need to change his job or his wife. In case of the wife, she has little recourse but to fall victim to a persistent neurotic suffering, unless she is one of those exceptions like Margaret. Margaret realized that she needed to be alone, to introspect, to relax, to rest, to meditate. In other words, she needed to shift gears to a lower one. She needed to surrender to the needed rhythm of her body and psyche. A spiritual guide helped her to recognize that.

On the other hand, there may be women who even in their advanced age need to live in the extroverted world of ideas, action, decision, and organization. They make good politicians and policymakers. They need to live their masculinity more directly than they have done before in a married woman's role. As long as they are content with this lifestyle, they are following their inner direction.

Lest it appear that women are the only ones who suffer from life's disillusionment, let me turn for a moment to the men's side of the story. I already alluded to a gradually forming discontent and anger among men in the '80s and '90s. Many husbands, lovers, and friends of the women mentioned so far began to resent being the understanding and supportive males so that their wives and colleagues could be self-actualized and fulfilled individuals.

John, 36 and married, wanted therapy not because his wife insisted, which is a common phenomenon. He wanted a male therapist, and I saw him for a couple of sessions before referring him to a male colleague. I learned a great deal during these two hours. His posing of the problem simply surprised me, as it was not very different from that of his female counterpart.

He was getting tired of being the understanding husband who chips in all housework, including childcare. For a while it felt good to be part of the current norm — the part-provider and the house husband at the same time. But, "Hell," he exploded, "I don't think I want to be all this. I am tired of being the good guy who pleases my wife's feminist friends. I find myself catering to their 'ideal,' which seems very convenient for them. But, I'm realizing now that it doesn't do it for me anymore."

He also hinted that many of his men friends are going through the same realization and becoming angry at this lifestyle. They don't dare voice it openly for fear of being called the old-fashioned macho males. These men apparently would not mind exchanging places with their fathers, who had clearer positions in the family and had the time to enjoy the football games with their male friends. John ended with a cliché to describe his situation. He felt castrated.

Unlike John, Michael, who is 45, came to therapy because of his wife's insistence. He mentioned this at the very outset and added that all his life he tried to please someone or other. First, the father, then the boss, and now the wife who is also the "boss." His wife, a successful businesswoman was very critical of his unassertive character.

"Yet" he said, "when we first met, she liked me precisely because of my 'gentle sensitivity,' as she called it then. After 15 years of marriage, she calls me 'a wimp.' I admit I'm not the most aggressive guy on the block, but I like myself and I don't see any reason to change now." To my question what exactly he expected from therapy, he could not respond at the time. Gradually, it became clear that all he wanted was some kind of confirmation from another woman that it was all right to be the way he was. After that he wanted to be left alone.

"I was influenced by the '60s ideal and was even a hippie for a while. We believed in love, not war, and ecological protection. We demonstrated against the testing of the nuclear bombs." Michael continued, "My wife hung around me and my hippie friends because she liked the way we were and what we believed in. Many of my friends are now successful yuppies who lost all their ideals and gentler sides. I suppose I'm still the same person I was then.

"When I married my wife, I admired her strength and conviction. Now, the same strength is hard to take. I feel like rebelling again, not just against her. ... Why can't a man be what he is? It seems he has to be always something someone else wants him to be — father, peers, wife." Michael trailed off with an expression more despondent than angry. He also lamented the fact that men today had so little guidance from other men. They needed a viable movement to stand up for their rights. Yet he was seeing a woman therapist and stayed on for three years. When he terminated, he was still married but was less dependent on his wife's approval. To his credit, he started a men's group in his home with six other friends.

Interestingly enough, Michael's wife came to see me several months later, and it was quite revealing that she wanted a change in the status quo of their marriage as well. She was tired of being the more dominant and more active partner. She no longer needed to be the "husband," as it were.

Some of my male colleagues corroborated that they, too, received similar messages from their male clients recently. My experience with John, Michael, and other male clients with similar concerns made me aware of how parallel the problems really were. If indeed men in the '80s and '90s were waking up to a reaction — often a raged one — against the feminist expectations, they perhaps were asking for the same goals as their wives were. Like women, they, too, wanted to find their own sovereignty, not to cater to someone else's expectation. The two examples above also tell us that the maleness in each man is different, and it needs to be lived and expressed differently in proportion to their feminine side. Otherwise, they risk being macho or over-feminized. Moreover, a man's process need not be separate from that of his wife's. One can complement the other, as it indeed happened in Michael's case. But for many, it may have to be separate. Several books explore these changing motifs in the masculine experience, *Iron John* (Bly, 1990), *Fire in the Belly* (Keen, 1992), *King, Warrior, Magician, Lover* (Moore, 1991).

Another question comes up. What then is the role of a woman in a man's journey for his self-discovery today and vice versa? In the traditional model, the hero's coming of age began by slaying the dragon or overcoming the negative aspect of the Mother. Women during the last half a century tried desperately to follow the same model to become independent of their mothers as well. Today, both men and women know that overcoming the negative aspect of the Mother is tantamount to a fruitless effort to overcome the dark half of one's own nature. The slain dragon not only remained in the unconscious but also returned in newer incarnations in every man's and every woman's life. As I unfold more life stories, it will be obvious that the old model is obsolete even for men. Where can today's women and men find guidance for the initiation to their womanhood and manhood?

I hope to answer these questions throughout this book. But first, I need to introduce a few simple concepts that will be the building blocks to our understanding of all these issues and concerns. These are psychological tools that will recognize and explain at least some of the contradictions and confusions the above stories convey. We hope to be able to detect where the traditional role models fail to be the carriers of proper expressions of our deeper needs. And, more importantly, what can we do to bring about conscious changes?

Archetypes

Earlier in the Introduction, I referred to a woman's inner masculinity. In the Celtic tale, the old witch demanded to marry the young knight Gawain as a price for offering her wisdom to King Arthur. Gawain is the personification of her masculinity — her inner potential, with whom she needs to be united in a "marriage relationship" so she can be delivered from her bewitchment. She then can live a normal life of a young woman with the potential of becoming a mature woman someday and be guided by her wisdom throughout her life. Conversely, Gawain as a man needs to face his ancient femininity, his wise but neglected and feared anima. He needs to surrender to her wisdom with respect before she can be his partner, his equal. In every woman resides the archetype of the Masculine, the male image and traits — her animus, which she projects on outer men and in the process realizes its presence within herself. The same is true of the Feminine archetype, the anima that is within a man's unconscious.

It was Carl Gustav Jung, the Swiss psychiatrist who reintroduced the ancient concept of the archetype[8] back to depth psychology. Archetypes refer to innate patterns that are expressed in emotions, images, and repeated human behavior. All typical human emotions and life situations that endure and are regulated by social norms and legal and religious institutions are archetypal.

The best representations of the archetypal emotions are divine figures. Ancient Greeks and the Indians, among other peoples, have pantheons full of gods and goddesses representing various aspects of our emotions and roles from mothering to killing, loving to hating, ambition for power to surrender, and much more. For example, the Hindu goddess Durga, who is widely worshipped in India, is a warrior, a wife and a mother. As a warrior, she kills the demon who threatens the universe with destruction.

In the Greek pantheon, one of the goddesses is Pallas Athena, who was born of her father's head and stands for reason, clarity, and battle. She protects art and civilization. She also sponsored the hero in slaying the Gorgon, the petrifying dark aspect of the Feminine archetype. Then there is Aphrodite, whose presence brings beauty and sexual love that can be reckless, unruly, and jealous. And Hera, who stands for the divine marriage, is always possessive of her husband and forever trying to destroy everyone Zeus favors. Similarly, many gods represent various aspects of activities and traits that are models for masculine nature or the Masculine archetypes.

Gods and goddesses as archetypal expression are appropriate because archetypes are transpersonal energies in our psyche that we do not own but are part of. For example, the goddess Aphrodite exists in all of us, but may manifest differently because of our personality and cultural upbringing. Therefore, by knowing the stories of the goddess or god of love, I may understand which aspect of this divinity is prominent in me and which in another. Mythology, which tells stories of the divine world, is attractive to even the most rational mind because by listening to them, we recognize our deeper nature and see many possibilities of being who we are. We also feel a heritage, a connection to the sacred world beyond the everyday mundane existence. For the same reason, religious rituals can be so healing.

What then happens to a culture where the pantheon of gods, goddesses, and demons evolved into a monotheistic one and eventually lost the emotional significance to the rational mind? This evolutionary development created a psychological vacuum because one God cannot hold multiple projections of human emotions. This crisis, on the other hand, created a consciousness that evolved our emotional life. Like Athena's birth out of Zeus' head, psychological concepts were born from the intelligent understanding of our experience. The divine figures, in the meantime, were repressed to the collective unconscious only to lurk in the depth of our souls and only to appear as dream images. Some of them are being reincarnated in modern shape and form like movie stars, rock musicians, and charismatic leaders.

The birth of depth psychology ushered by Sigmund Freud a century ago was one of the greatest events of our time because it also began the era of a consciousness about ourselves, our unconscious life, about finding meaning of our emotional suffering, and eventually a desperate search to reclaim the lost gods and goddesses. In this latter endeavor, C.G. Jung was a pioneer who paid serious attention to the complex and contradictory inner world in order to understand the neurosis of modern times. He discovered how eager modern people were to recreate a divine world where they would be able to project not only their puzzling and threatening unconscious but also the transpersonal aspects of themselves — both divine and demonic.

The ancient concept of the archetype was thus rediscovered by Jung to explain some of the emotional experiences he observed among his patients, people around him, and in himself. In everyday life, we may be shocked by a crisis and awed by a dream image that is numinous in its impact. Often such a profound dream or feeling can bring a person to analysis because she/he is puzzled by this intrusion into the consciousness. This intervention, which can be called divine, is no less powerful than visions experienced by the ancient prophets and saints.

For example, a woman woke up with a dream in which a golden snake was wearing a crown made of gold and beautiful gems. She was so awed by this dream snake that the only way she could describe it was that it was a profound religious experience. The snake lingered in her memory so strongly that she had no choice but to treat the snake as a divinity. She was inspired enough to go into a full-fledged research on world mythology and discovered that in some parts of the world (India and Myanmar) the snakes were (and still are) worshipped as divinities. This dream and the experience afterward changed her life in a way that she was forever grateful to the snake that she calls her god. She did a painting of this unusual serpent and hung it on the wall of her bedroom, where she sees it every morning and every night.

The transpersonal quality of the archetype that transcends actual experience can be felt in everyday relationships. For example, when I try to talk to my mother about a problem I have with her, both of us are influenced by an autonomous atmosphere that is beyond our grasps. Part of this, of course, comes from our upbringing, the cultural expectations, the role — ideals that we may or may not fully like. It is an atmosphere also of instinctual patterns carrying strong emotions and images none of us can control or understand. It is as if we are not just one specific human mother and daughter — but part of many mothers and many daughters before us and after us.

We, mother and I, are part of a collective experience although individual at the same time with our specific issues and problems. In this regard, I may also find similarities between me and the Greek goddess Kore, the way she related to her mother, in the Demeter-Kore myth. Thus, I am a woman who is part of a collective psychology as well as a transpersonal life that transcends both the individual and the collective. When recognized, this knowledge is an experience that deepens our relationships and our existence. Otherwise, life becomes just a routine with literal implications and experience of merely here and now.

Linda, Pam, Susan, and millions of others today need to recognize this truth and try to reconnect with their archetypal worlds. Only then will they be able to reclaim the water of life that has been bogged in the tangle of role stereotypes, which are cut off from their archetypal roots. Before we move to how Linda or Pam can go about doing this, I need to differentiate the concept and experience of the archetype further.

Archetypes, therefore, are at the foundation of three dimensions of one's identity: (a) personal — consisting of the conscious personality grounded in biological instincts and archetypal patterns; (b) collective — created by the cultural tradition that teaches roles and norms and directs one's place in society; and (c) the transpersonal — one's connection to the transcendental and the eternal aspect of life, the realm of the divine.

I also need to distinguish between the Feminine and the Masculine archetypes, which are psychological styles of being present in both genders. However, the archetypal Feminine in a man (the anima) may be experienced and expressed quite differently from the femininity in a woman

45

because a woman by her biology and upbringing has a closer connection to this archetype. The same goes for the Masculine archetype in a woman.

For example, for a woman who is primarily a mother and feels comfortable being one, a significant part of her identity is rooted in the archetype of the Mother. The Mother archetype permeates through Mother Nature — the essence of the maternal instinct in both its constructive and destructive manifestations. She perceives life (perhaps unconsciously) in the model of a relationship between the mother and the child whom she nurtures and cares for. Yet as in the story of Jesus and Mary, she also must let go of her son, no matter how painful. Women who are not biological mothers may experience the power of this archetype as strongly in other relationships or in indirect ways, as Cheryl did in her work with African children.

By the same token, the Masculine archetype, the animus in a woman, is experienced and expressed quite differently from the masculinity in a man. By virtue of their biological heritage, men are connected to the Masculine archetype more directly.

Masculine and feminine are also root metaphors for the fundamental polarity of all conceivable pairs of opposites in both natural and symbolic worlds — mind/body, spirit/matter, conscious/unconscious, right/left, sky/earth, and many more. Almost all languages tend to categorize nouns, both animate and inanimate under two genders. These opposites, like the two genders, are bound together. They are two sides of the same coin. This archetypal pairing of the two opposites is beautifully depicted in the image of the Hindu divine syzygy of Shiva and Parvati combined in one body. The Chinese concept of yang/yin and the Tibetan yab/yum are similar conceptual symbols of the same pair.

Within each woman and man, there exists a yearning to bring the two opposites (symbolized by the masculine and the feminine modes) together. This is an archetypal need and is the most difficult psychological task. Yet, only through the union of the opposites we can transcend the opposition and become one with God or reach the eternal bliss that Eastern religions call Nirvana. Nowhere do we see this complex task played out more poignantly than in the real lives of women and men as another syzygy in both outer and inner worlds.

Speaking of the outer life, a woman's self-image depends primarily on her biological identity, which must be grounded in the feminine archetype. Her identity as a woman is also enhanced by her cultural values associated with femininity as opposed or in complement to masculinity. All cultures distinguish between the gender roles and try to instruct the boys to become men and the girls to become women.

Femininity (or masculinity), therefore, is a complex style of being that combines the instinctive and archetypal with the socially learned as well as culturally adaptive behavior of a particular time. For example, women in America in recent decades have been doing multiple jobs that were associated with the male gender earlier. Since the '90s, along with being a wife/mother and a homemaker, over 65 percent of American women have worked in every field, including all branches of the military. What this society defined as typically feminine in the past is expanding to include many unfeminine (as defined earlier) qualities and activities. Earlier, what her society defined as masculine had been repressed inside her and now constitutes part of her lived masculinity, her animus. This is the cultural dimension of the animus, which will change over time as the values and styles in a culture change.

The development of a woman's animus (personal aspect of the archetype) depends on her relationship to her father, father figures, and other male members of her family as well as the cultural image of masculinity at the time, and her ego (conscious psychology). Her ego has to relate consciously to the animus for the animus to have any value to her. Typically, when a woman is unconscious, she experiences various aspects of her masculinity through projections on men and things and ideas that represent masculinity in her culture. If she remains unconscious of her inner masculinity too long, the animus becomes a complex and creates destructive symptoms, such as severe problems in relationships with men and society. She may also identify with the unconscious animus and become an Amazon with competence and skill but a lost feminine soul.

The healthy development of a woman's personality depends not only on her ego development but also the ego's gradual coming to terms with her unconscious archetypes — both Feminine and Masculine. In order to achieve that, she first needs to know how these archetypes manifest in her everyday life. Moreover, she needs to differentiate among the personal, cultural, and transcendental dimensions of the archetypal experience so that she can diagnose the roots of the problems correctly. Then the ego is better able to incorporate and change toward a balance between her various sides.

Unless consciously recognized and integrated, the potentially health-giving and creative archetype becomes a destructive complex. In everyday life the unlived animus can interfere in various ways. It may take the form of admonishing criticism (the collective judgment), and driven and compulsive actions or comments, and even uncontrolled sexual acting out or fantasies involving diabolic figures such as the devil or Dracula. In the cases described earlier, we saw other kinds of expressions. Cheryl's life was dominated by a professional animus identification, making her a competent doctor but a very unhappy woman. She could not form any relationships either with other men or women or with herself. In a sense, she was married to her animus.[9]

Addictions, obsessions, eating disorders, and general body-problems seem to come from the wounded Feminine archetype. Since the archetypes use the means of culturally accepted behavior and symbols to express themselves through life, it is possible to trace back the destructive symptoms and neurotic behaviors to either the Masculine or the Feminine archetypal roots. However, the personal life history is a major contributing factor.

Determining the origin of the neurosis depends a great deal on the knowledge of the symbolic and behavioral expression of the two archetypes. This task, however, is complicated by the fact that the cultural definitions and expressions of femininity and masculinity change over time. These changes are better captured in the symbolic and creative expressions of the culture at a given time, such as mass media, art, literature, and technological innovations. The typical complaints and symptoms that bring people to therapy also reflect such a change. But first, we need to look back at the cultural and psychological history to determine how the evolution of patriarchy in the West gradually managed to tilt the balance between the Feminine and the Masculine archetypal experience in individual as well as collective lives.

Struggle Between the Sexes

Healing projections on divine figures seem no longer possible today – to believe without questions is old-fashioned and regarded a sign of weakness. The emphasis on enlightenment and consciousness in modern Western society promotes a skeptical and rational attitude toward everything, including the supernatural. This attitude, shared widely by men and women alike, results from the spectacular achievements science and technology have made throughout the last two or three centuries. While the unprecedented material progress promised more and more comfortable economic standards, an increasing number of people, and women in particular, became aware of the price they have to pay. Let us briefly look at the historical and psychological antecedents for this development.

The Goddess Disappears – The Historical Background

In *The Origin and History of Consciousness* (1954), Eric Neumann recounts the gradual evolution of consciousness in the West as it developed on the collective and transpersonal level. He describes cultural instances that correspond to his psychological findings and are symbolically expressed in mythology. Because mythology expresses the collective beliefs and fantasies about things that lie beyond material existence, it is the clearest manifestation of the collective archetypal projections a society has. The moving symbolism of mythology becomes renewed over time, whenever the individual psyche needs to find its roots in the social consciousness by establishing an emotional link.

Comparing the mythological images throughout history and even prehistory, Neumann shows how the Western patriarchal system established itself by subduing and overcoming the devouring and fearsome aspects of matriarchy. As a symbol of masculinity and ego consciousness, the fight with the mother dragon becomes the hero's struggle for self-liberation. The growth into adulthood appears synonymous with the growth away from the mother, from nature. This developing masculine principle then symbolizes culture that lies apart from, and nearly opposed to, nature and the feminine principle.

Similar observations are made by the early sociologists and prehistorians. Lewis Mumford in *The City in History* (1961) writes:

> In the early Neolithic society, before the domestication of grain, women had been supreme. ... It was woman who wielded the digging stick or the hoe; she who tended the garden crops and accomplished those masterpieces of selection and cross-fertilization which turned raw wild species into the prolific and richly nutritious domestic varieties; under woman's dominance, the Neolithic period is pre-eminently one of containers; it is an age of stone and pottery utensils; of vases, jars, vats, cisterns, bins, barns, granaries, houses, not least great collective containers, like irrigation ditches and villages. ... Woman's presence made itself felt in every part of the village: not least in its physical structures, with their protective enclosures, whose further symbolic meanings psychoanalysis has now tardily brought to light. Security, receptivity, enclosure, nurture. In Egyptian hieroglyphics, 'house' or 'town' may stand as symbols for 'mother', as if to confirm the similarity of the individual and the collective nurturing function.
>
> (page 25f)

The goddess myths of the Middle East, the Mediterranean, and Asia reflect the same concepts of nurturing and organic growth that follow the inner and outer rhythm of nature. The goddess adjusts to the unfolding of life without fear; she does not concern herself with principles but with utility, not with right and wrong but with the practical business of reproduction, propagation, and annihilation. The remnants of terracotta statuettes of fertility goddesses at the archaeological sites of Sumer, Asia Minor, and India testify to the early ritual importance of the mother goddess. Goddesses such as Kali and Medusa stood for archaic destruction, while their benevolent counterparts protected creation as if to maintain the natural balance between death and life. Morality in the sense of superego or social conscience did not exist, except in some form of an internalized taboo. Like nature, where mutual killing sometimes restores order and balance, these goddesses were amoral.

The evolution and gradual innovation of technologies, along with the domestication of plants and animals, began to change the picture.

The density of population increased, and people had to learn to live side by side. They moved from the natural rhythm of procreation and annihilation to a cultural order in which a sense of social morality became essential. Cooperation among people was necessary to defend against natural calamities, predatory animals, and, later, other fellow humans. Then, cooperation was quickly followed by competition, warfare, and organized defense. All these needs found their concrete structural expression in walled cities where families and clans began to live, protected and subordinated by a higher external order or organization. Establishment of political and economic systems, along with the organized utilization of natural resources, became evolutionary necessities.

Goddesses were pushed away to the recesses of dark woods, to the corner of household shrines, and, ultimately, to the unconscious. They soon were replaced by male sun gods and, finally, with the advent of Christianity, by a male trinity that put the mother of Christ in a subsidiary position. As a major part of the Western world came under the influence of Protestantism, religion became further male-oriented by defining the godhead as the only and ultimate spiritual figure. This development created an emotional distance among the human worshippers, and women in particular, of the male god, which could not be reconciled to the feminine way of being by even the highest degree of intellectual consciousness. Paradoxically, the same alienation from the feminine principle seems to have encouraged an intellectual evolution that led to various technological innovations leading to a material progress unprecedented in human history.

The Goddess is Replaced — The Psychological Parallel

While the archaic feminine mode was based on organic balance and followed cyclical patterns, the new masculine perception was built on perpetual innovation and progression in a linear way. The replacement of goddesses by gods went hand in hand with substituting the emotional and amoral rhythm of nature with a logical and moral conscience of the organized culture. Even today, many women experience an instinctive resistance to social morality, bureaucratic organization, and mechanistic principles, which are the necessary foundations of modern social evolution and of all technological innovations.

Feminine inclinations as they are mentioned here refer to a woman's instinctive feelings and not to what she learns to become. Of course, a modern woman may believe strongly in living by masculine modes – something she has learned and is proud of because man, and his style of being, are considered superior in her society. Her developed animus (or the masculine aspect within herself) helps her to achieve the special fascination she feels toward the masculine world. This fascination points to the archetypal basis of her attraction. A modern woman is challenged by running her life alone, taking care of finances, learning auto mechanics, playing masculine sports, working side by side with men in the world of technology and every other area of specialty. She has learned to argue logically and scientifically about the mystery of her body and soul. Yet, there are many who find it very convenient and comfortable to have a man or husband take care of all these tiresome details, allowing her to be herself without giving in to the pressure to compete with men.

Interesting examples of what I mean by the archetypal basis of the fascination for the masculine mode can be seen in many social customs and rituals of primitive societies. Because it is not natural for a woman to be like a man and, because women are attracted by this forbidden world, both women and men are allowed to dress and act like the other sex in routine rituals such as *Naven*, observed among the New Guinea tribes.[10] Similar observances take place among civilized societies when a military football team dresses up as women for entertainment. Established night-clubs in many parts of the world feature acts in which men impersonate women or vice versa. Even in the best-known gay nightclubs like The Pinocchio of San Francisco, the most popular performances are the ones by impersonating women or men acting as the opposite sex.

The development of a predominantly masculine self-consciousness as the foundation of modern Western civilization had to go hand in hand with an increasing alienation from the feminine mode of life. The resulting chasm culminated in splitting the conscious from the unconscious and the rational from the emotional in both collective and personal lives.

Perhaps this process of segregation of the sexes with an increasing dominance of the masculine over the feminine goes back to the time of disappearance of the Neolithic goddesses. Thus, the masculine mode continued to replace and repress the feminine mode of being and the resultant experiences within the female psyche could be akin to the unlived characteristic male behavior, since women could not live openly as men and vice versa. In fact, the segregation of the sexes on the external level was necessary for the survival of women and men as they adapted to changing socio-cultural environments. One wonders further if this process, then, had given rise to the archetypes of the contrasexual in the unconscious: animus in women and anima in men. Animus and anima, or the masculine and feminine archetypes, are personal as well as tran-spersonal, individual as well as collective, as the following quote shows.

According to C.G. Jung, the maternal (feminine) and the paternal (masculine) modes each have distinct psychological implications:

> "The most immediate is the primordial urge of the mother;... she is experienced by the more or less unconscious child not as a definite, individual feminine personality but as *the* mother, an archetype charged with an immensity of possible meanings ... in the unconscious the mother always remains a

powerful primordial image, colouring and even determining throughout life our relations to woman, to society, to the world of feeling and fact, yet in so subtle a way that, as a rule, there is no conscious preparation of the process."

And,

Just as the mother archetype corresponds to the Chinese *yin*, so the father archetype corresponds to the *yang*. It determines our relations to man, to the law and the state, to reason and the spirit and the dynamism of nature. ... He is that which moves in the world, like the wind; the guide and creator of invisible thoughts and airy images. He is the creative wind - breath — the spirit, pneuma, *atman*."[11]

Femininity Devalued — The Splitting of the Archetype

As Western societies evolved with the necessary division of labor defined by sex, the repressed contrasexual archetypes developed in a parallel fashion. On the conscious level, the trend was to put men in power to run things efficiently on the outside, leaving women to deal with things on the inside, at home and away from the outer world. Except for matters concerning childbearing and child-rearing, an attitude of devaluation soon became associated with women's activities and abilities. Masculine objectivity and rational analysis were considered to be more useful tools than the feminine approach of intuition and looking at situations in totality, especially in political, economic, and technological matters. This degradation of the feminine principle, along with the disappearance of the goddesses from the religious sphere, severely affected the balance between the sexes and their archetypal needs for centuries to come.

The tension between the sexes later developed into a struggle, with women feeling strong animosity and mistrust toward men. Indeed, the battle of the sexes is not new and not only present in the West. But the manifestations of this archetypal struggle took on special expressions and trends in the West. The swings of the pendulum seem to be characterized more by competition and struggle than cooperation and compromise, and synthesis or balance still remains to be a far cry.

Art, literature, and mythology expressed this struggle in symbolic forms throughout the centuries. Some aspects found expression in social roles, supported by cultural norms. The image of polarized dichotomy between the venerable and pure mother of Christ and the deplorable witches, for example, has been quite persistent. The split between respectable mother/wife and the ignoble prostitute prevails even today, not only within the psyche of men but also in the self-image of women themselves. A woman who represses the prostitute and emulates the virgin mother will end up with an identity that is not only incomplete but also innocuous. While Immaculate Conception and virgin birth are rather far removed from her reality, body awareness and sensuality seem to belong to witches and prostitutes and have to be rejected from her conscious self-image as well. By devaluing the feminine archetype that includes birth and death, women were left with only the role of being good mothers who are life-givers only, not destroyers. They are trained and disciplined to feel only goodness, and natural anger or hate remain totally repressed, taking the form of a powerful shadow.

The typical woman of the Christian West strove to become always kind, harmless, innocuous, and agreeable, in the process of which she lost her shadow and therefore her real connection to her archetype. The repressed shadow remained with the witches in European fairy tales and folk legends — a latter-day proliferation of the original dragon. Like the dragon, these witches, too, got killed or conquered by the hero. This split of good and bad in the feminine archetype created a curious dualistic attitude toward body and sexuality, as we find it later in the simultaneous practice of sexual Puritanism and promiscuity in the American society. In Europe, the same dualism finds its expression in the age-old practice of extramarital affairs and legalized prostitution. The object of respect (wife/mother) and the object of sexual desire (prostitute/witch) thus became separated.

However, in the unconscious recess of the psyche of both women and men, the compensation emerges through the fascination for the undesirable and the dangerously negative. Even though the culture and religion may emphasize the positive images of men as fathers, guides, priests, and protective heroes, women are attracted by the dark bandits of romance literature. In men, the fascination with the vampire is still alive, and the image of the devil, attractive and repulsive at the same time, appears in many modern Christian women's dreams and fantasies.[12]

On the social level, both sexes agreed upon the appreciation for masculine values for a long time. For generations, women played the roles of the dependent and inferior species who needed men as protectors, providers, guides, and even rulers. They learned to admire men's abilities and talents in running intricate social and political organizations; they admitted that men possessed more objectivity and level-headedness in restraining and controlling chaotic feminine emotions. At the same time, women never quite understood why men behaved the way they did. While showing open veneration to men and men's systems, these women also nurtured a hidden sneer, mistrust, and even disgust at men's approach to life, especially ambivalent sexual practices.

Jessie Bernard (1966, '73), a prominent American sociologist, showed in several studies how women after years of marriage were often frustrated when they discovered real weakness in their husbands, whom they believed to be like sturdy oaks. These feelings, often suppressed and repressed, were handed down to the next generations of women. Even today, a daughter may be advised by a mother or a grandmother as to how childish and helpless men really are and how she has to deal with this delicate situation. She must learn to accept the dilemma of living with a weak man on whom she must also depend. The sense of devaluation among women themselves perpetuated for generations. A series of surveys was conducted among 900 college students during 1968, 1970, and 1972 (Broverman, D. M. et al.) on the topic of sexrole stereotypes at the time. The result was impressive: Even among university students, not only were the stereotypic masculine and feminine traits similar and agreed upon by both sexes in all three surveys, but women and men also agreed on the relatively higher value of masculine traits. In 1976, I, myself conducted a similar survey among 50 Swiss students of both sexes at Zurich University, and the results remained very similar. Another study among Midwestern high school students in the U.S. showed that if they had a choice, the majority of the girls would like to be boys.

In addition, this devaluation influences many areas of social and cultural life. Interesting observations have been made by linguist Robin Lakoff (1975). She found that colloquial English language has no comparable expressions referring to men for derogatory terms such as bitch, witch, broad, and hag. If anything, they are neutral or positive, such as the word bachelor as opposed to spinster. Old feminine virtues such as endurance and sacrifice changed into their negative variants, implying weak manipulation and martyrdom. A "sacrificing wife" is in fact a guilt-provoking martyr, and only a woman becomes the proverbial nag!

Women of the most recent generations learned to survive by instinct and to hold onto some power within their own world by sometimes fighting masculine domination with the help of feminine means. These feminine means often appeared surreptitious and questionable to men. In turn, men learned to be afraid of such "manipulative" moves and never quite understood or trusted women's ways. In defense, they often became offensive and oppressive, controlling women with their own means such as laws, rules, and even physical force. Yet, both remained interlocked by their bonds of ambivalent emotions such as love-hate, trust-mistrust, and their social and emotional needs for dependence on one another. Each lacked the tools, sensitivity, and reference points to understand and sympathize with the other.

It is in this regard that the idea of the contrasexual within the personality of each sex can be so useful and vital, since the outer struggle of the sexes is exacerbated by the lack of understanding and sympathy between the sexes. Sympathy can be generated only through the knowledge and inner experience that stem from the connection between the conscious ego and the unconscious archetype. When a woman feels a masculine persona inside her, she can no longer be either a blind worshipper or an enemy of the men outside. Similarly, a man also can liberate himself from extreme fascination for, or fear of, his anima and women in general. One of my main objectives is to show how vital a part this connection plays in the process of a woman's adaptation to her society, to her outer and inner world. So far, we can define the quality of the collective animus as it exists in today's Western societies as (1) a product of patriarchal, historical developments with all the implications, and (2) characterized by primitive emotions because of its being unconscious and unlived. The workings of such collective animus can be discerned in many areas of customary social behavior and within institutional setups, such as marriage.

The New Consciousness — A Double-Faced Janus?

The most significant collective behavior in which the long-dormant animus is projected can be found in the institution of marriage and in women's socio-political movements. In both areas, the animus is experienced through identification with collective ideas and ideals of the times. In its negative aspects as well, animus most often is projected onto marriage partners and political adversaries. While the significance of marriage and the women's movements may not be of the same degree for a woman, both areas have certain things in common. Women have a strong influence on both as they themselves are influenced by the way marriage evolves or the women's movement develops. While a woman's attitudes and views affect her relationship with her husband and family, a change in her attitudes may very easily result from the prevailing ideals espoused by the movement.

There are cases where marriages become unstable after women have been exposed to a college education or revolutionary ideas. From 1970-72, I conducted a research on the psychological factors of divorce in California. Several former husbands told me with a lot of resentment that after their wives began to take courses at the university or listened to their feminist friends, the status quo in their marriage began to break down. The wives began to question their husbands' authority and seemed reluctant to make any efforts to compromise. The wives, on the other hand, complained about how static and rigid the husbands remained, how they refused to acknowledge changes in the social atmosphere or in the wives' newly found needs. The women's liberation movement, then nearly a decade old, had a lot to do with these developments, offering many women a first inkling of realization of their psychosocial condition. The impact was far-reaching. By listening to radical views that even threatened her marriage, a woman felt connected to a community of her sex. She no longer felt isolated within the walls of her marriage and family. This change in women, of course, slowly began to influence men and society at large in direct and indirect ways. C.G. Jung, in his paper *Women in Europe*, published originally in 1927, very astutely hinted at the increasing restlessness of the women of Europe even at that time. They could no longer be satisfied with the old-fashioned patriarchal marriage where they remained either contained or became a container. This "loosening of the marriage," as Jung called it, was only partly a natural evolution of emancipation from a symbiotic marriage that restricted a woman's personal development.

A great deal of this change had to do with the economic and techno-logical progress following the two world wars. Most significant of all was the invention of oral contraceptives, which allowed women in Europe and the U.S. to control conception and frequency of pregnancy. Maternal instinct for many women became synonymous with consciously controlled behavior instead of being regarded as a natural condition. The rapid progress in domestic technology (electric cooking range, washer, dryer, vacuum cleaner, dishwasher, blender, etc.), as well as a market-centered economy of the American version of capitalism, turned the world of women into one of compulsive consumerism. Now women could not only do their household duties in a shorter time, but they also controlled childbearing much more efficiently than ever before.

This newfound freedom from destined motherhood and strenuous housekeeping, however, came with a price. Women began to lose the satisfaction of being nest-builders, wives, and mothers. The challenge of building a home and family no longer rested in a woman's ability to organize creatively. As machines began to take over, housekeeping became nothing but chores that demanded mechanical rather than instinctive and creative abilities. Women themselves started to devalue domesticity. Therefore, a woman's instinctive needs to be a mother and a partner in building a home remained increasingly unsupported by the postwar Western societies, despite the unconscious and even conscious messages from older generations who still stressed marriage and motherhood as a woman's ideal goals in life.

The postwar economy, with its increased economic standards and higher cost of living, aggravated this contradictory situation and pushed many women into the job market. These women were trained mostly like men since the so-called feminine professions of teaching, nursing, and secretarial work could not accommodate all the job seekers. Effective birth-control measures allowed women to be free to go out to work. Increasing competition with men forced more women to pursue masculine skills provided by an educational system that did little to encourage feminine qualities such as intuition, feelings, and expressive emotions as part of their educational skills and job training.

As women remained less satisfied emotionally, a realization began to take shape: They had gone headlong to eat the fruit of masculine consciousness, including its virtues of objectivity and skepticism. A skeptical and rational attitude thus permeated nearly all human experiences, including the most mysterious feelings of love and religious belief. For a while, women even became proud and confident of their abilities to deal with the outer world like men. They could prove to themselves and the men around them that they were as capable and good as men in doing what men in American and European societies had been brought up to achieve. The masculine attributes and attitudes that women of older generations had mistrusted were now successfully indoctrinated into their daughters and granddaughters.

Separation from the Mother — A New Independence: Identification with the Animus

Already in the 1960s, the image of the accommodating, gentle, and self-abnegating wife had become obsolete in America. Books published much later such as *Kiss Sleeping Beauty Goodbye* (1979) and *Cinderella Complex* (1980) show that many women of that period reacted strongly to such ideals. The hot, albeit controversial, discussions of these books in the '70 and '80s demonstrate the birth of a new myth turning against the sacrificial Cinderellas and the innocent and dependent Sleeping Beauties who needed a Prince Charming for their awakening and deliverance. Nancy Friday's *My Mother, Myself,* which was published in 1977 clearly voiced the need of American women to separate from their mothers' myths and ideals if they hoped to become self-fulfilling individuals.

The women who became adults by the '70s worked hard to attain the self-worth and independence their mothers had been deprived of. This meant, among other things, rejection of marriage and of men as the providers of economic and social security, which led to the sad rejection of man's love and caring. Professional commitment became synonymous with emotional commitment, implying a woman's occupation was the only basis of her identity. Women began to choose not only between marriage and work but also between love and work. A ridiculous visual example of this rather simplistic solution to a complex problem is a billboard I saw on many roads of London in the '80s showing a couple of executive women wearing masks of men's faces among a group of men in business suits. The caption read: "Women Can Be Successful Too."

On television, the widely popular afternoon soap operas portraying women characters clinging to the old image of sacrificing wives/mothers continued to satisfy a group of old-fashioned female viewers who were nervous about the new politics. However, there were also new serialized productions like *The Mary Tyler Moore Show,* for example, where the heroine is a young and competent professional woman who remains unmarried and independent despite occasional attachments to men. Movies like *The Games Mother Did Not Teach Us to Play,* released in the early '70s, centered on a woman who proved her self-worth heroically by holding onto her executive position despite enormous obstructions caused by male colleagues and her husband. She seemed to have no alternatives but to choose her profession over her marriage. The husband in this movie showed a fair amount of understanding and cooperation in the initial stage of his wife's search for independence and the issue of a woman's self-actualization. But in the end, her exaggerated professional ambition drove him to suggest a separation. In his eyes, she has been too busy with too many board meetings on too many weekends.

Those women who in the '60s and '70s tried to combine profession with affection for men were too afraid of the emotional commitment. Besides, they already had surrendered to their jobs, and men had become afterthoughts. The juggling act of how much of herself to give to whom created a very unsatisfactory situation for a working wife/mother in that era. Some tried "open marriage" and "honest communication" with partners only to find that these strategies were not that relevant to the mystery of emotional bonds. The worst shock came about when many of these couples who practiced honest, open marriages were caught unaware by primitive emotions of jealousy, mistrust, anger, and revenge. The negative emotions they thought they could control by intelligent understanding and well-meaning ideas tore marriages apart when they exploded with the intensity of volcanic eruptions — an archaic revenge of starved instincts and emotions indeed!

This trend to cling to the myth of independence at the cost of marriage, motherhood, and love for the opposite sex gripped America and a few of the West European countries until the '90s, when a reaction formation set in. Psychologically, a woman became identified with the masculine archetype in its collective aspect, which often turned negative because of its lack of balance within the feminine principle. The question remains: Why did women have to identify with the animus rather than their own archetype when they needed a secure identity so badly? Why did women have to be successful men first in order to become respectable women?

The answer lies partly in the process of degradation of femininity as it had evolved for centuries in the West. As we saw, the immediate situation for women of that era arose out of their shame of inheriting the wounded and neglected feminine image from their mothers and grandmothers and several generations before them. In desperate search of a new identity, they grabbed the only possibility offered by the culture and society. But the fact that they fell into a new false identity was not apparent to them until time passed for their observations and experience. By the '90s, even the heroic women began to realize that imitating the male heroes in their journey of separation from their mothers might not be the right path for them. Only a logical and extroverted materialistic analysis was not enough to understand the deeper problem of women. Even in the Western tradition, the road to consciousness and independence for women could not be the same as that of men, although along with risking and incurring a heavy price, women also gained a temporary improvement in their social and economic positions.

Revenge of the Mother: Emotional Suffering Begins

Fortunately for some of these women, the glory of success after a while failed to bring the promised satisfaction. The realization that professional success and independence from imprisoning marriage and pregnancies caused an emotional void began to dawn on many of them. In the well-argued book *The Cost of Loving* (1984), the author, Megan Marshall, who herself underwent similar challenges, documents how the career women of America faced the painful realization of the price they paid for their freedom, which remains a chimera still. They were no longer locked up in unsatisfactory marriages but were steeped in dry and impersonal professional lives. Emptiness and loneliness awaited them at the end of the long road of struggle. Let's look more carefully at the situation after nearly three decades of liberation and feminist movements by women of the West to improve their fate.

The Dynamics of Marriage

By the end of the '90s, something new began to happen in the dynamics of marriage. Because of the identification of a woman with the collective animus along with the increasing overlap of the two worlds of men and women in education and careers, the separation between the sexes was reduced considerably. The animus can no longer be projected onto the husband as it used to be in a traditional marriage, where the symbolic structure with a division of labor by sex roles made the projection possible and necessary. This so-called symbiotic marriage, however, worked only up to a point. Erich Neumann, in his insightful article "Psychological Stages of Feminine Development," shows how such a marriage could easily be a perfect ground for the gradual sacrifice of a woman's natural matriarchal consciousness — her femininity in the archetypal sense. Neumann asserts:

> "Her life and interests are reduced to the merely personal, even
> to the purely material, and an animus psychology in imitation
> of the masculine now appears which represents a capitulation
> to the masculine and a degeneration in place of the matriarchal
> spiritual productivity peculiar to the feminine." [13]

This particular brand of 'merely personal' and 'purely material' existence was quite common in old-fashioned marriages of a generation or two ago. Many of these women remained steeped into a totally material life where husband, children, and house all became possessions. When unsuccessful with such possessions, which constituted their only identity, some of the destructive plots hatched by these women were indeed very archaic and destructive. Their unconscious life allowed both the primitive destructive feminine and the negative animus to work in collusion. This destruction was worse because women who brought them about were often unaware of their own motives and actions. However, such unconscious destructive forces seem rare in the urban West of today. Education and identification with the animus (in both positive and negative senses) make it impossible for a modern woman to be totally unconscious of herself.

Husband's Role

What Neumann calls "matriarchal consciousness" is almost antithetical to today's educational system and lifestyle that modern Western women have embraced. Women who are outside the pale of this new consciousness are only a minority. Today, when a woman marries after several years of college or university plus a few years of professional experience, the relationship with the husband is not always clear-cut. To a large extent, he no longer needs to carry her projection of the active, protective provider animus. This is further complicated by the upbringing most Western men had and are still exposed to. The changes that took place in a woman's life during last half a century are far greater compared to the changes in men's lives, which have begun to change only recently and that, too, mostly as a reaction.

Men in America until the current generation had been brought up by the model and ideal of the "tough, aggressive guy" who brought home the bacon, providing physical and economic security for the family. This widespread masculine ideal also had a strong influence from adventurous cowboys, who were modern knights and were always ready to shoot the enemy to save damsels in distress. The immense popularity of American Western movies with tough characters acted by the likes of John Wayne can be explained by the same archetypal masculine model mentioned above. The other desirable component to the aggressive male was the romantic attribute, something akin to the medieval knights again. Hollywood movie idols such as Clark Gable, Humphrey Bogart, Gary Cooper and many others were aggressive yet handsome men mostly on horseback wooing and courting beautiful, lovesick and dependent, albeit intelligent, women. Social roles and educational training were geared to uphold this aggressive, adventurous, romantic lover who was at the same time the providing protective father figure to the whole family.

With such a role model, modern men of the last three or four decades had been faced with women in marriage and love relationships who now suddenly do not need this machismo in their men, at least consciously.

For many men, this confusion is explained by women's undesirable transformation emasculating them from their ideals of strong providers. In their eyes, women ceased to be feminine enough to be desirable and respected. This opinion seems stronger among European men than among men in America. Hilde Binswanger, a Swiss psychotherapist, in her article "Development in Modern Women's Self-understanding," (1975)[14] mentions how a man in the changing atmosphere finds it difficult to literally carry a business executive woman in his arms! The symbolic implication of this statement may explain, among other factors, why so many career women in the first part of last century remained unmarried.

This problem of a missing link between the partners of a marriage will continue unless and until men themselves begin to be aware and develop the femininity within themselves – a need as vital as the development of the animus in women. Moreover, as long as a woman continues to identify with the animus, the outer man ceases to be essential as her psychological complement. In the meantime, however, her matriarchal consciousness (in Neumann's terms) continues to be developed. Thus, marriage dynamics turn into a stalemate, leading first to inner and then to outer separation of the partners, as reflected in consistently rising rates of divorce. It is also interesting to note that the majority of the divorce initiators happen to be women – a fact that already appeared to be valid as early as in 1927 (C.G. Jung)[15]. Divorce lawyers in both America and Europe testify to this trend.

Divorce and Women

The reason so many more women take the initiative to start divorce proceedings lies in their qualitatively different kind of dependence on and expectations of the marriage. Marriage as an institution gives a woman her primary identity in adulthood. She finds a socially accepted, legally protected, and culturally commendable framework for realizing her instinctive and spiritual self. Ideally, a marriage offers the best workable (even when it does not work) stage for her self-realization through interplay with the opposite and complementary sex. A man's primary identity derives from his position at work. His roles as a husband and father take a secondary position. For a woman, the relationships with her husband, children, and relatives by marriage are vital for her emotional development and security. She moves to her spiritual plane through her personal relations within the family, which also offers a favorable ground for fulfilling her instinct of mating, nest-building, and mothering.

So, when the marriage fails to offer her an emotional basis, it becomes redundant to her archetypal needs. That is why many women, even in their advanced years, can dare to be alone after years of marriage. They claim that it is better to be alone than lonely within a marriage. Even though marriage is an equally favorable vessel for the husband's development of his anima, he may be less aware of this deeper psychological need or, when aware, values it less. His primary satisfaction comes from his relationship with abstract ideas and objective goals, and often projection of the anima onto newer and younger women. In an evolved man the same anima may develop into a creative muse guiding him to fulfill his creative potentials.

In a woman, however, the estrangement from the archetypal roots, and thus from the feminine self, can create a loneliness so strong that it can even make her sacrifice the social and financial security of marriage. The repressed animus, which lived only unconsciously through projection on the husband, turns negative and creates disturbance within. This disturbance actually leads to the breakdown of the projection, separating the woman from the protective vessel of marriage. This is an archetypal urge, like the hero's need to separate from the mother to gain further consciousness. In women who have long been alienated from their feminine roots, only the masculine archetype, with its characteristic aggression, can make the first step through separation.

For example, a woman of 50 (among many others) after 30 years of marriage wanted to be divorced from her husband, who fought hard not to grant it. When she succeeded after a long legal battle and a substantial loss of money, she suddenly looked and felt alive. To the great embarrassment of her grown children, she began to show interest in all sorts of masculine, aggressive sports usually attractive to younger people. She obviously had to live a fresh version of her animus for a while.

The critical junctures of life at which outer conditions and triggering factors develop into the need for divorce usually appear either within five years or 25 years of marriage. Whereas divorce in the early part of marriage may be a direct result of the withdrawal of positive projections on both sides, the later divorce is complicated by additional factors. The crisis that hits all people at the middle of life, irrespective of outer situations, becomes more difficult if the marriage as a vessel has lost its containing or supportive qualities. Conversely, the midlife crisis, in both biological and spiritual aspects, poses an additional challenge to a marriage that already has to adjust to changes, such as children growing up and leaving.

For a woman, the "empty nest" produces more difficulties if she has been nothing else but a wife and mother. After years of engaged mothering, some women cope with the released energy by taking up some outer activities or professions. However, unless a woman is aware of the real situation, no amount of outer activities may solve the problem of emotional loneliness. Her maternal love and involvement may need a different channel for expression. She may even go back to becoming a wife again, in a different way. This is the most difficult adjustment in the life of a woman who has been married many years and mothered children. Marriages break at this point because she needs to develop herself, without the husband, unless he can change and adapt to her needs as well as his own. In the past, the continuation of the mother's role to the grandmother's used to solve some of these adjustment problems, but the geographical separation between parents and married children increases in today's more mobile and less tradition-oriented society. Grandparents are not needed to provide continuity to the past in a society that values obsolescence and the worship of youth.

Aside from the "empty-nest" syndrome, the other common triggering factor for a divorce initiated by the woman is the love triangle in which the middle-aged husband cheats on his middle-aged wife. Most commonly, he does so for a much younger woman who boosts and renews his self-esteem at this critical point of his life. Without going into an analysis of the man's anima problems in midlife, it is quite safe to say that a betrayal of this kind has a significant impact on the rejected wife. The shame and anger of betrayal might have a positive effect in the way that the suffering could lead her to reestablish contact with her own shadow side – which is what the younger woman may really represent. Yet, this is only possible if she allows her shame and anger to evolve into pain and suffering, rather than turning it into bitterness and revenge, aiming at nothing but to fight the husband.

In either situation, breaking off a marriage can precipitate consciousness and growth in a woman who fails to achieve it within the marriage. I do not intend to support divorce, but the ever-rising statistics of divorce in the West as well as in other countries only indicate that it seems wiser to accept the fact before analyzing its implications.

Whether married or divorced, by going out into the world, a woman may experience the collective aspect of the animus for the first time, tasting the excitement of a world run by ideas, money, business organization, and power in a way life inside the home does not offer. She can establish a connection to the masculine archetype on her own rather than through her husband. She becomes impersonal and part of the wide world after having been exclusively personal for a long time. An increasing tendency to go back to some professional training or even just voluntary work reflects this trend among middle-aged women in both America and Europe.

Women's Movement

While marriage is an ancient institution, serving as a stage for the battle and balance between the sexes, women's socio-political movements are fairly recent innovations. The first organized movement among women probably began with the suffragists in England around the middle of the 19th century, followed by movements in America and other countries. The leaders of these movements were educated and courageous women who regarded the political and economic equality of women to be essential prerequisites for their personal development. Today, women's movements have several branches — some emphasizing issues such as equal rights and equal pay, and others questioning more psychological situations.

Again we see an outer and an inner parallel, an extroverted and an introverted approach to further development. It is interesting to note that the latter groups are labeled "consciousness-raising" groups — a consciousness that may be, unconsciously, close to what Neumann calls "matriarchal." Most often, however, these women take a rather extroverted, masculine approach to the problem, and often their course of action appears to stem from an identification with masculine traits and views. They are intent on fighting the male world on male terms because, in their minds, this is the only way to win. They organize, mobilize, and act with enormous energy to fight the government or the establishment, which may very easily carry the projection of the oppressive, tyrannical, and negative masculinity within themselves. Women who belong to the radical political branch of these movements take an Amazon approach, fighting men with men's weapons and sacrificing their feminine strength and position in the process. The mechanism of the victim's identification with the oppressor's traits works perfectly until at least some of these fighters become aware of the futility of such battles. Getting the government to pass a few bills in their favor does not seem to satisfy the real needs that are at stake.

This awareness dawns on some in the same way it does on professional women when they suddenly feel an emotional emptiness in spite of all the outer successes. Very often the radical feminist group becomes as aggressive as its adversaries, only to hide a wounded self-image. When this repressed image finally surfaces, women may express it through another unconscious act by becoming lesbians — a phenomenon observed sometimes among radical feminists. While they reject men totally on the conscious level, their unconscious search becomes a reconnection with the feminine shadow or a lost mother's love that has been neglected for a long time and remained unavailable. In the privacy of therapy such unconscious dynamics can come out in some cases. In what more desperate way than through sexual love for the same sex can this need express itself? The battle between women and outer men is also a battle for deliverance of woman from the possession/domination of their negative animus, or the inner men. From this point of view, lesbianism may appear to be a solution, and the emotionally supportive group helps these women to avoid living a life that is totally barren and loveless.

There are also less radical branches of the women's movement. They take a middle path by organizing for women's causes and reestablishing emotional connections through group meetings and encounters. This may very well be seen as a compensation for the previous rejection of the Mother, or the feminine archetype in all its aspects. Indeed, one of the noticeable changes among American women since the 1950s brought about reduced competitiveness and increased cooperation with other women. A genuine sisterhood seems to have flowered among many women during the last few decades.

Readjustments of the extreme attitude among some of the leading women's liberationists are interesting to note and tally with several other findings mentioned earlier. An ardent feminist leader of the '60s, who marched in many demonstrations and drafted many bills for equal rights surprised me when I met her 10 years later. She confessed how tired she was of all the talk about equality of the sexes. Now she wished women learned to be unequal to men and to not feel guilty. I wondered whether this was not another sharp swing of the pendulum in the typical American style.

But then other voices began to join hers. The publications of the two well-known feminists Betty Friedan and Germaine Greer testified to similar changes of mind and heart. Betty Friedan's *It Changed My Life* (1977), which went through 10 successive editions, was published over a decade after her best-seller *The Feminine Mystique* (1963). While her first book sharply criticized the old, mysterious feminine image, this later one is an honest confession of the dilemma women face in trying to grasp their real identity. If loving a man makes a woman feel better, that is her identity. With true feelings, Friedan espouses the need for relationships in a woman's life and how emotional commitments constitute a woman's identity.

In *Sex and Destiny: The Politics of Human Fertility* (1984), Germaine Greer goes even further by advocating motherhood as being the only solution to a woman's identity crisis. This is indeed a great change from Greer's earlier scathing criticism against anatomy being a woman's destiny. After spending years encouraging women to free themselves of predestined motherhood, Greer, then in her middle years, came back full circle to claim that motherhood establishes the link between a woman and her past and future; it offers her a lasting identity.

It remains an open question whether these changes in some leading feminists' viewpoints resulted from their own biological maturation that reversed ideas and opinions of youth, or whether they also reflect a general attitudinal change. Friedan's plea appears to be supported by much younger women, as in *The Cost of Loving: Women and the New Fear of Intimacy* (Putnam, 1984) by Megan Marshall. The dilemma of choosing between work and love brought many professional women of this age group to the painful realization of a severe emotional loss.

Yet, a group of women remained quite alienated and maintained an extremist stand. An example of this can be seen in the recent controversy over who controls reproductive technology. An extremist group of women fights men to gain control over all the latest technological means concerning reproduction, beginning with contraceptives and ending with test-tube babies, frozen embryos, sex selection, artificial insemination, and surrogate motherhood. Is this, then, an attempt to control destiny by controlling anatomy after all? By denying man's sexual involvement, have these women not been seduced by the worst male aspect, the efficient and manipulative knowledge of physiology, which resulted in a technology invented, executed, marketed, and profited from by men? A sad irony indeed! A detailed treatment of this controversy, taking the radical feminist stand, has been published by a group of women specialists, *Test-Tube Women: What Future for Motherhood?* edited by Rita Arditti et al. (1984).

Surrender to Suffering: New Identity?
New Consciousness?

By the late '80s, women began to realize the extent of the emotional price they had to pay for their professional success. Within 20 years of the late '60s, a shift had taken place from an identification with the animus to the search for feminine roots. Volumes of archaeological, psychological, and theological research on the lost goddesses and their significance for modern women exemplify this development. Extroverted outer battles and aggressive arguments began to be replaced by an introverted and introspective search for insights. For the first time in Western history since the Enlightenment, women began to look for inner enemies rather than for outer ones alone. All this led to a gradual acknowledgment of a kind of suffering that originated from the pain of losing the Mother, losing the emotional and instinctive base of oneself.

The collective expressions of such feelings are peace marches and demonstrations and protests through cultural and emotional means, such as punk music and unisex clothes. These symbolic and pacifist means of protest aimed at political decisions that may destroy the ecology and psychology of humanity are emotionally effective. They touch the deeper chord of feelings as it manifests itself in the feminine archetype, where processes are defined by natural balance and cyclical movement.

In its ideal role, the masculine consciousness questions before feeling, judges with objectivity before acting, and keeps contradictory factors in mind before judging. But to obtain fair results, objectivity and impartiality must be tempered with feminine emotions such as pity, mercy, and compassion. Then only wisdom is born out of the union of the masculine and the feminine modes. Women who ate the fruit of masculine consciousness to counterbalance the very personal, subjective, and totally dependent existence of their grandmothers had no choice. The collective life of the last half of the 20th century has been dictated almost totally by the masculine archetype, in both its positive and negative aspects. Religion, politics, education – and the men and women living with them – all were rooted deeply in this mode.

Women who separated from their mothers to become self-fulfilled individuals found recourse in the collective aspect of the animus, since its negative side was paramount in creating the disturbance and frustration that led women to question and struggle, and ultimately to a new consciousness. They questioned precisely the state and conditions their mothers were content with, but within the next 10 years, this skepticism gave way to emotions of loss, sorrow, and vulnerability, rather than just frustration and anger. This new insight indicates a swing of the pendulum toward the feminine pole again, but on a different level than ever before. Outwardly, both women and men are confused about their real identity vis-à-vis one another as well as one's own self. The institution of marriage reflects this confusion best through its multiple variants of household arrangements during the '70s such as communes, communities, family houses, etc. Yet, after five or seven years, many couples opt to get married and set up their private households despite today's relaxed legality regarding children born out of wedlock. Confusions in relationships between the sexes find expression not only in high divorce rates, but also perhaps in mass movements for homosexual and lesbian preferences.

We can only hope that out of all this chaos a new balance will emerge between the sexes. If insight and inwardness lead women and men to the reconciliation with their contrasexual archetypes, the outer struggle eventually will lead to peace. Women in the West have already shown the first act of courage by consciously acknowledging their emotional needs as women, something they and nearly all women had lost or repressed for a long time. This realization must be brought to coexist with the animus, since after all it was their animus that led women toward a new consciousness through a tortuous path of illusions and disillusions, success and failures, pleasures and pains.

Until now, for both men and women, consciousness derived from the hero's killing of the dragon, representing the negative aspect of the feminine archetype. By searching for the feminine identity, today's women try to reverse the pattern and hope for a new feminine consciousness that both kills and protects, loves as well as hates. Because women know themselves better now, they also know that the dangerous dragon cannot be annihilated, that it lurks inside all women and all men, albeit in different ways. If not consciously accepted, the destructive part of the Mother-goddess would devastate civilization with such vengeance that no hero could stop it. Signs and warnings of this are visible in schemes of political madness and man-made climatic change that point toward the probability of global destruction.

If indeed it is the angry and violated femininity that is about to strike back at our one-sided civilization, women now carry a graver responsibility to help men in rebuilding and recreating a constructive balance. A woman can do so when she is first a woman in her body and soul, and then in her social and cultural roles, and when she acknowledges that her power can both create and destroy. Then only can she combine the woman and the man within herself and help man to live in balance. As part of Mother Nature, hopefully she knows more about true balance than anyone else.

ENDNOTES

5   By 'Cultural Archetype' I like to refer to the representational expressions (art, language, dream and fantasy images etc.) of archetypal energy which are conditioned by the specific cultural heritage. It is different from the term 'Cultural complx' introduced by Joseph Handerson along with 'Cultural Unconscious' and further elaborated by Thomas Singer, Samuel L. Kimbles et.al. of California. Cultural archetype is not yet become a complex. By using the word archetype I like to emphasize that the archetypal energy is available to the individuals via their cultural symbols to establish healing connection hopefully before the energy is captured by the complex which can control the ego often negatively.

6   For the background material please see Manisha Roy (1976, '93), *Bengali Women*, Chicago: Chicago U. Press

7   Murdock, Maureen (1994) *The Hero's Daughter*, New York: Fuwett Columbine, page xiv

8   Although it was the Greek philosopher Plato who first put high value in the concept 'archetype' as a metaphysical idea, Jung admits of borrowing the term from St. Augustine, the medieval philosopher (*Collected Works*, vol 8, paragraph 275.) Even though described and referred to several times since 1912, Jung uses the term for the first time in 1019. He defines it many different ways depending on the context and the Jungians do the same. I like the following brief

description: "The archetype is a psychosomatic concept, linking body and psyche, instinct and image" in Andrew Samuels, Bani Shorter and Fred Plaut: *A Critical Dictionary of Jungian Analysis*, London: Routledge & Kegan Paul, 1986.

9   For more information on Cheryl's life story see Manisha Roy's article "Developing the Animus as a Step Toward the New Feminine Consciousness" in *To Be A Woman* (Ed) Connie Zweig, Los Angeles: Jeremy P. Tarcher, Inc. pp.137–149

10   'Naven' is a customary ritual among a Balinese tribe called Latmul in which women and men act as their opposite sex. This ritual was first observed and recorded by Gregory Bateson (*Naven*1936) and later by his wife Margaret Mead.

11   Jung, C.G (1931) *Collected Works* vol 10, paragraph 64-65.

12   For a comprehensive discussion of this topic in English literature and life, see Kate Millett (1969 and 2000) *Sexual Politics*.

13   See Erich Neumann: "Psychological Stages of Feminine Development" Tr. by Rebecca Jacobson in *Spring* 1959, New York.

14   Binswanger, Hilde (1975) "Development in Modern Woman's Self-Understanding" C.G. Jung Memorial Lecture (private circulation).

15   Jung, C.G. (1927) "Women of Europe" *Collected Works*, vol 10, paragraphs 236 - 275.

CHAPTER 2

Indian Experience

Another Version of the Balance Between the Sexes

In contrast to the West, the process of psychological evolution of Indian society seems to be characterized by a predominance of the feminine archetype. Masculine patriarchal development did not quite succeed in replacing the feminine importance of the Neolithic period despite numerous invasions and rules from the West throughout Indian history. Matriarchal dominance has managed to survive alongside with a very well-developed patriarchal social system structured by the highly complex hierarchical organization of a caste system unique to Hindu India.

It may be an interesting but difficult task to speculate why and how such a development could take place in India and some other parts of Asia and Africa. Whatever the geographical, historical and cultural antecedents were, this unique evolution is also exemplified by the living mythology of numerous divine figures and their life stories with a strong emphasis on female divinities.

Mythology: The Goddess and the Gods

It seems appropriate to begin discussing the situation in India with the world of mythology. For a majority of the Hindus, everyday life and the mythic world of the gods and goddesses are closely linked. The former is not only modeled after the latter but also receives sanctions, guidance, and healing from ritual observances venerating the divine world. At least the majority of the population likes to believe so.

In a country where life and economy are predominantly dependent on soil and earth (70 percent of India's population is engaged in some form of agriculture or related activities), it is not surprising that the goddesses who look after fertility, flood, drought, and perilous animals should be important. These goddesses who are associated with malevolency and destruction — an experience not uncommon in this country — are even more powerful and popular among the worshippers than their male counterparts. Usually, the male gods do not represent quite such basic elements of destruction and death. These goddesses who are believed to bring on natural calamities such as disease and death can also cure them. They can be appeased by routine worshipping in everyday rituals. Their stories and tales are told and retold from generation to generation, and a living mythology, which is also written in 18 volumes of the *Puranas*,[16] narrates adventures, attributes, life stories of the gods, goddesses demons, sages, sacred beings, and even sacred places.

Out of hundreds of versions of myths connected to particular divinities, I shall choose only those directly relevant to our topic. The goddess whose beauty, glory, and power are described in a major part of the mythological writings mentioned earlier, is Durga.[17] In one version of her story, Durga was born of a powerful king, who never approved of his daughter's choice of husband, the unconventional god Shiva. Yet, Durga had meditated thousands of years to win Shiva's love. Once, Durga's father held a big sacrifice and invited all the great kings and queens and bigger and lesser gods and goddesses, except his own daughter and son-in-law. When Durga heard this, she was extremely hurt and insulted and decided to attend the gathering uninvited. Shiva objected, and they had a long argument. Durga, out of frustration and anger with both her father and her husband, became increasingly angry and showed her Kali form (the destroyer), to whom Shiva bowed down and agreed to her going to her father's home. Kali is the dark version of total fury of Durga that was born out of necessity when the goddess was commissioned by the male gods to go and fight the invincible buffalo demon who was threatening the whole universe, in a bloody battle of ten days and ten nights. Durga with her ten arms of weapons offered by the gods had to invoke all her strength born of anger and fury to be able to fight the demon and finally subdued him. Kali is worshipped as a separate figure in Hindu pantheon who is not only able to conquer a ferocious and destructive adversary but also is the Mother principle that keeps the balance between creation and destruction, good and evil in the Nature both outer and inner. There are other myths of her origin, some of which show her separate existence in other traditions.

Going back to Durga's story, her arrogant father did not welcome her to his home and even cursed her saying that he'd welcome her with open arms when she became a widow! This was too much for Durga to take, and she died or committed suicide according to one version. Her raw, feminine fury cost her life, and her divided loyalty to her husband and her father is the same existential conflict that all Indian women must live with. Yet, according to the tale, it is her husband that she must listen to; otherwise huge calamities, including death, can occur.

In another incarnation – when Durga as a young girl named Uma is married to Shankara, a new incarnation of Shiva – her mother pines for her visits and sends her husband to go to Uma's husband to ask permission to have her back with her parents for a few days. Shiva agrees that she can go and visit with their four children for only four days if he, too, accompanies them. This four-day visit by the married daughter to her parents is celebrated in the biggest religious festival in Bengal and in some other parts of India every autumn. She is the married daughter who visits her family in a festive reunion. She is also the mother and protector to her worshippers. After four days of the festival, the image of Durga is immersed in the sacred river, the Ganges (or any river), and her worshippers know that she is now gone for another year till her return again in next autumn.

Durga is also the warrior who killed a buffalo demon. Once, all the gods in heaven were in grave crisis because an invincible demon born of a buffalo threatened to destroy all three worlds — heaven, earth, and the underworld. Paradoxically, he became extremely powerful by the blessing of the gods themselves because of his perseverance in deep meditation for many years! No god knew a way to combat this calamity, either alone or even together with other gods. As the council of gods sat fuming over this frustrating situation, the accumulated energy of their frustrated anger gave birth to a blazing fire and Durga, the fair skinned goddess with 10 arms materialized from the potent energy of the frustration and anger of the gods. As this powerful goddess was born out of male wrath, her 10 arms were decorated with weapons offered by the surprised but delighted gods. Now they knew that the demon would be vanquished. Durga rode a lion and went out to fight the buffalo demon. After a ferocious battle, she killed the demon and saved creation — indeed, an interesting reverse parallel to the Western myth of the hero killing the dragon.

As mentioned earlier, while fighting the terrible battle with the buffalo demon, Durga became black in anger and became Kali (the word has the same root as that of the word 'black' or *kalo*), and only then could she kill without hesitation. The same Durga became Kali once again when she was angry with her father and her husband, and showed her husband this formidable divine form to impress him. The energy out of which Durga is born and which is used to kill and protect is called *shakti*[18] a Sanskrit term that is also used as one of Durga's many names. *Shakti* is the vital energy that kills, protects, acts, and moves, as opposed to the passive energy of her husband, Shiva, which represents stability and containment. Shiva needs Durga to activate his passive energy, and he must contain her active energy if it goes too far.

In the same goddess we therefore can experience both the protective and destructive energy in the "Durga" and "Kali" versions. Thus, both these positive and negative poles of the feminine archetype are embodied in this Hindu goddess. Born out of masculine emotions, she can also be close to the archaic feminine destructiveness; yet, she seems to be endowed with a meditative and evolved introversion and a well-developed Eros for her husband. The myth is alive and is reincarnated again and again in newly created images by the sculptors who specialize only in making divine images every year that Durga's worshippers keep a ritualistic, intimate but devotional contact with this collective anima figure.

The annual celebration worshipping Durga, along with the elaborate nature of the ritual, emphasizes the transcendent quality of the divinity, as well as a strong identification by an Indian woman as a married daughter returning to her parents' home. Many Hindu girls are given one of the many names of their goddess and are brought up with the projection of the divinity by the family members, as it were. Their fathers and other men may even address them as "mother," as Durga herself is addressed by her worshippers. Hindu women are believed to possess *shakti*, the divine power that can protect as well as destroy, unless they are contained by their Shivalike husbands. This divine power, which is protective and destructive in its negative aspect, is archetypal, therefore transpersonal and beyond individual control. The cultural and social roles can only humanize and temper such ingrained archetypal power by dictating women's behavior through acceptable norms. One such framework is the institution of marriage, where the husband carries the projection of the animus such as the god Shiva, who had to contain Durga's fury and destructive aspect within their marriage.

A Hindu woman's living connection to the warrior goddess who kills the evil yet powerful demon and is also a loving wife and a mother-protector is of enormous importance. For women with such religious and mythological roots, the experience and the projection of their animus seem to follow the model of the divine marriage between Shiva and Durga and its turmoil. In India, the image of women on a human level corresponds to the mythical account described above. Anthropological observations report that women in remote villages are considered to have a touch of divine power, *shakti*, by the people around her. Such power also helps her husband and her family in many respects. However, she must nurture this power by remaining sexually chaste and by fulfilling her feminine roles prescribed by her family, her caste, and her culture. She must be enduring and ready to sacrifice. These latter qualities enhance her *shakti* and enhance the good fortune of her husband and the family indirectly. A man also possesses a bit of this feminine *shakti* (one of the anima qualities) and he, too, can increase this power by rigorous training in highly disciplined yoga that involves strict dietary and sexual restrictions. But mostly, he benefits from his wife's *shakti*, and that is why for an ordinary man, having a wife is essential because only a few men can increase their *shakti* through rigorous yoga. However, in order for a man to become an ideal husband, he also needs to become a yogi. The god Shiva, Durga's consort, is both a yogi and a lover, therefore an ideal householder.

In rural India, women are sometimes considered physically more capable than men. They not only bear and rear children and keep house, but also work in the fields alongside the men in the severe tropical climate. Women are considered closer to the divine world and in many households are entrusted with the daily worshipping of the household deities. The husband, in turn, must know how to tame the raw fury in his wife's nature, and this conjugal interplay finds expression in the social system where the outer norm emphasizes the superiority of men that counterbalances the religious superiority of women. On the behavioral level, a separation between the worlds of men and women is maintained. While men rule the outer world, women rule the inner. The public is separate from the private. This interplay between masculine and feminine, like the conjugal drama of the divine couple, is portrayed in numerous other ways: in epics, folk tales, modern mass media, and literature. The powerful, yet suffering and persevering woman who waits patiently for her temporarily wayward husband is a character in many stories, novels, and films. She ultimately defeats the temptations of demonic forces, and her husband comes to the realization of her power, her *shakti*.

Parents and elders in India often bless their young daughter by saying, "May you marry a husband like god Shiva." The word *Shiva* literally means "good" and "auspicious." He is one of the great Hindu trinity - Brahma, Vishnu and Shiva -- and represents (like one aspect of his wife) destruction, while Brahma stands for creation and Vishnu for preservation. Shiva can destroy creation through his frenzied cosmic dance, yet he is the god always approached for protection when creation is threatened by some kind of calamity or other. Like his destructive wife, Kali, he knows how to protect because he knows how to destroy. Once, in a churning of the ocean activity between the gods and the demons who were looking for the nectar, Shiva volunteered to drink the poison that came up before the nectar because neither the gods nor the demons wanted it. Shiva held the poison in his throat and since then has a blue throat. He is a god of opposites and paradoxes. A yogi with matted hair adorned with snakes, he is the most virile of lovers and husbands. He is friendly with thieves, the insane, low-class people, witches and imps, smokes hashish with his friends, who take care of the dead. He wears a decoration of the feminine moon on his hair and rides a masculine bull. He has no permanent abode, unlike other gods, yet he is the ideal householder with his wife Durga. Although unconventional, he is a faithful lover and allows his wife to retain her divine power, but contains her destructive anger. One such as Shiva is considered to be an ideal husband for a Hindu woman.

The other important Hindu god that women worship and is relevant here is Krishna, a god who is the antithesis to Shiva. While Shiva represents the ideal husband/lover inside marriage, Krishna represents the ideal lover outside of marriage. While a young girl worships Shiva in the form of the lingam (the divine phallus) to be blessed by a husband like him, a woman worships Krishna only in her advanced age. Krishna stands for the ecstatic yearning for love that is experienced outside of marriage, in incest, and in love for one's god.

Krishna is also known through various versions of his life story in many forms. As a cowherd, he played the flute to entice all women of all ages away from their households to the world of ecstatic love for the lover, who creates bittersweet love of pain, longing, jealousy, despair, yet ecstasy and devotion, finally leading the worshipper/lover to her god, her animus. According to a folk myth, Krishna married 1,600 women to save them from permanent spinsterhood, had six princesses as wives and indulged in a lifelong love affair with Radha, an aunt by relation. Besides being the lover who breaks the boundaries of marriage and incest, he is also a warrior, a trickster, a mischievous tease, a great politician and the wise adviser about just warfare to his friend Arjuna, the warrior hero of the Hindu epic *Mahābhārata*.

A god with charming blue complexion, Krishna symbolizes many other aspects of the masculine archetype as well. Despite his irresistible charm, women in India know that having a husband like Krishna would be impractical, if not disastrous. As a collective animus figure, he provides a poignant allegory of the deep longing for the union with one's god and one's soul, a union that may never come to fruition but remains a quest. Psychologically speaking, for a Hindu woman, the god Shiva carries the projection of her personal husband/animus and the god Krishna carries the image of the impersonal and transcendental aspect of the archetype.

From her early years, a girl in a typical Hindu Indian household is brought up to know and to believe that marriage is the final and most desirable goal of her life. Marriage is the major framework where the couple can act out the anima-animus projections following the model of the divine couple, Shiva-Durga. Even the Hindu wedding ceremony, with its very elaborate rituals and customs, emphasizes such identification with the divine couple.

Indian Women Today: Interplay of Life and Archetypes

As a young girl, she is brought up by her female relatives to learn to become an enduring, suffering but powerful woman who must go through the difficult experiences of childbirth and adjustment to the husband's family. The *shakti* that she inherited from the goddess Durga can be kept alive only through fulfilling her family roles dutifully. She must aspire to be a good daughter, wife, and mother, since only through these roles will she continue to realize her divine power. By being a good daughter, wife, and mother, she also ensures her good name in her family and society, thereby ensuring her positive identity.

By valuing the roles that are rooted in instinct and tradition both, a woman's archetypal needs such as mating, nesting, and mothering are satisfied. Her instincts need not be sacrificed for her social and cultural identity, as has been the case in the lives of many American women today. Despite the alarming demographic index and strong propaganda in favor of birth control, being married and being a mother still remain two of the most desirable and respectable goals for most Indian women of all classes and backgrounds. Moreover, like the goddess, who is a wife, a mother, and a warrior, there is no apparent contradiction for a woman between the role of a householder and a military career, for example. However with increasing urbanization in a globalized world marriages are not always founded on the archetypal example of the divine couple. Couples in the largest cities like New Delhi and Mumbai show increasing number of divorce which can be as high as 40% of the total number of marriages. However according to the census report of 2017 (the latest available) the percentage of divorce in the whole country is only 1.1%.[19]

This indeed seems to be true. Many Indian women today are in careers in the so-called man's world, from abstract sciences to physical labor. Intellectual or academic achievements do not seem to clash with women's roles as wives and mothers. To begin with, a woman is encouraged by her father and father figures to go for education, a trend that began perhaps with the Christian missionary activities and later with the coming of the British, when upper- and middle-class educated men began to enjoy social gatherings and activities in groups of both sexes. Not only did men in many cases encourage their women to go out into the world and educate and enlighten themselves, but India also has a unique history where the first women's movement was led by men, such as Gandhi and other reformers and political leaders.[20]

Of course, in the lower strata of the country, women are married quite early and work very hard physically either in the fields or in the factories. Among the very poor, education is not as relevant or essential for either men or women. Women in modern India, except for the very wealthy (about 1 to 5 percent of the total population), may have to work for economic reasons alone. Women who have some skill and education know that they must not usurp masculine power. In fact, they seem to enhance their careers by remaining within their feminine style of existence. Qualities, such as the ability to negotiate, to organize on concrete and practical levels, to be tolerant, and to serve and not being overly ambitious seem to help advance their careers. One well-known and successful woman medical doctor told an anthropologist once that the secret of her enormous success as a doctor lay in her ability to *serve* her patients. She considered herself a "servant" to her patients. If women do not compete with men, men in India not only allow but seem to encourage women to climb high in professions. Women must, however, act within the expected sexual norms and behavior. In case she does not, neither her male colleagues nor the society will protect and respect her.

If a woman's husband carries the projection of her Shiva animus, her other male relatives, and even her male colleagues, help her to realize the teasing, flirtations, attraction for her Krishna animus. Even as a little girl, she is spoiled by her male relatives with whom she plays games of emotional manipulations while they tease and indulge her. This playful and pleasurable world offers her an escape from the hard reality of the women's world where duty, sacrifice, and suffering predominate.

In her marriage, where the usual custom of separation between the masculine and feminine worlds (until recently) creates some distance, some of the problems of a marriage where the two partners live within an intimate and close space may be absent. On the other hand, some women in the urbanized upper strata of Indian society may be brought up with similar expectations about marriage as their Western counterparts. This happens because of their education and exposure to the mass media, which focuses on the aspirations for a better standard of living by consuming cigarettes or cars that are made for couples who are made for each other, as the billboard advertisements announce at every street corner. Most of these couples are struggling for a better economic standard while the couples in marriages of the wealthier urban milieu may develop marital problems not too different from those of couples in Western cities.

Frustrations that are likely to result from the practice of traditional marriage are not always experienced by all women, partly because of the ample indoctrination in their roles where a wife must adjust, adapt and endure to acquire a good name for herself and her family. Secondly, she is often quite preoccupied in running a household where more people depend on her organization, service, and affection than her husband alone. She not only accepts the situation but even enjoys the compensations that such an arrangement may offer in terms of intimate relations with other members of the family who may satisfy her various emotional needs. She may even develop very intimate friendships with her husband's younger brothers or cousins, or even his friends who pay devoted attention to her. Rarely do these contacts develop into sexual intimacy. The need for a one-to-one sexual love relationship outside marriage is not desperate because she is not lonely. Her involvements with other members of the family, whether they live together or not, add to and complement, as it were, her relationship with her husband.

Sanskaar and *Shakti*

The religious ideals and images of Shiva-Durga' s marriage and Krishna-Radha's love outside marriage remain the unconscious archetypal background in the psyche of married Hindu women. The value of chastity in marriage has its double foundations in the belief that sexual commitment to one's husband enhances her *shakti*, her innate power, and the ideal of the devoted love of Durga for her husband, Shiva.

While all this may be quite unconscious in the psyche of a Hindu woman, what really guides and dictates her actions and behavior on the conscious level is her *sanskaar*, an Indian word without a precise English translation. *Sanskaar* combines dogmatic ideals as well as customs and norms that perpetuate the practice of the ideals. The power of *sanskaar* constitutes a sense of security and the strength one acquires in one's culture and society by submitting to it. Thus *sanskaar*, while restricting, also permits an identity in one's culture and tradition over time and space. That is why *sanskaar* is very difficult to shake off because it is "in one's blood," as the Indian expression so aptly describes.

Without knowing it consciously, an Indian woman also knows that the real romantic yearning and its fulfillment can only be experienced in a love that is forbidden and incestuous as the love between god Krishna and his aunt by marriage Radha. One cannot expect such love from marriage with a human male. Such love is possible to realize in the love of the unattainable god, her animus. As a mother, her intense involvement with her son often takes on the color of her love for the god Krishna, sometimes worshipped as a child god, who charmed women of all ages even when he was a child. In her declining years, when she begins to lose her importance in her roles as wife and mother, her *shakti* seems less relevant, and her Krishna animus may carry her away to her quest for her god, her ultimate goal as a woman. A human figure, a "guru," or a religious guide, may carry such a projection at this time. Strong cultural and social support help her to realize this role, since by being involved in religious pursuits, a Hindu woman of advanced years brings prestige to her family and to herself. In some cases, her feminine *shakti* continues to be active, and she remains a mother figure. A matron of this kind may be more feared than respected. Some women seem to combine both roles until the role of the matron-mother recedes, gradually leaving her to her religious involvements.

While this may be the general pattern, there are women who occasionally rebel out of strong frustrations. If such frustrations find expressions in sexual relations outside marriage, the family and immediate society may pretend as if nothing happened and let the affair run its course. Whether it is tolerance or just fear of scandal or both, somehow affairs are rarely talked about openly, and the marriage moves on as if extramarital affairs ultimately have little to do with the marriage. One can also argue that the affection, tolerance, and respect, if not romantic intimacy, that grow within a traditional Indian marriage may be strong enough to allow love outside marriage without threatening it. The physical separation between the worlds of men and women in a traditional family may also allow the necessary deterrent against the contempt that breeds from familiarity and intimacy. A good example of this arrangement is found among the wealthy all over the world where husbands and wives have separate worlds of work, interests, and even intimacy. Their marriages are often socially intact.

In the case of India, it is not really possible to pinpoint the actual reasons of marital stability (divorce has been almost nonexistent until the 21st century) or even the actual practice. Intimate matters of life are not easily shared and talked about even among family members. My own observations as an anthropologist lead me to suggest that rebellion against the traditional *sanskaar,* pertaining to appropriate role and behavior within one's family in the form of extramarital affairs, is not so common or known to others. On the other hand, among the poor, such events may be handled more openly by direct confrontations between the partners followed by reconciliations or rare separations.

This is not to say that marriages do not dissolve in divorce. Incidence of divorce among the urban middle class is increasing. But the number is still quite low and is confined to only 1.1percent as mentioned above. As in the West, divorce results more from other reasons such as emotional or physical cruelty of the in-laws in a joint family than sexual infidelity, which often is the result, not the cause of marital problems. If a couple drifts apart in values and attitudes and ceases to have strong feelings of love and affection, divorce may not be the only solution in India, unless the family and society also cease to give support. Consideration for children, habits, fear of social scandal, and, more importantly, the security and support of the family may weigh heavily against a decision for divorce. On the other hand, divorce may be inevitable, not so much because of the loneliness the partners may feel within their marriage, but because of other family issues like continued cruelty by the family members on the married woman. The other possibility only exists in a city life, where the couple has lost both the containing security and the censorship of the extended family as a deterrent to divorce. Moreover, both partners need to have enough education and skill to be economically independent. Behind the decision for a divorce, the couple or one of the partners must also have the acquired value for independence and individualism, which are not relevant qualities in a traditional family system. Tolerance and acceptance of life's problems along with an attitude to share one's pains and pleasures, as well as income, are the foundation of traditional family systems in India. Although begrudged, these qualities seem to be still part of the clinging *sanskaar* in an Indian personality.

Marriages that develop into strong, intimate relationships are many. The bonds between the partners seem to combine affection, respect, and strong faith in the married and family life, which has its archetypal roots in the divine marriages. In traditional, or even modern Indian marriages, verbal communication on conscious level and understanding of each other's needs and compromises are less important than tolerance and acceptance of the partners even with their flaws.

The Westernized and educated section of the Indian population lives in the few urban centers and constitute about 20 percent of India's population of over a billion. This group came under the direct influence of the Western education and value systems through nearly 300 years of British rule. This is also the group that led India in the freedom movement against the foreign rule and laid the foundation for an independent nation committed to a democratic political system based on a free-market economy modeled after Western models. Influence from contact with Western rules and education over several centuries resulted in a strong bent toward materialism and a rational approach to existential problems, especially among men who were the first to come in contact with the Western education and value systems. Yet, despite this exposure for centuries, Hindu tradition rooted in the irrational and imaginal worlds of mythology and feminine psychology seems to persist, creating inevitable obstacles to the rational and material goals of this relatively new nation.

It is indeed an interesting paradox that the political leaders of India, who are committed to a British-style parliamentary democracy and a rapid economic growth based on heavy industries and free trade, are chosen by an electorate, the majority of whom are illiterate and vote for the candidates they love and adore as they adore their gods. Their judgment and selection are not rational but emotional. Yet, the same leader whose picture is worshipped among the divine figures in a household shrine is also assassinated by another kind of irrational emotion. The pervasive practice of corruption on nearly all levels of governmental bureaucracy in India shows a lack of morality that defeats all legal and moral standards. Occasional outbursts of chaotic violence lack organized plans and strategies, and may be termed more archaic and feminine in the negative aspect of the archetype. It is interesting that some terrorist groups are known to have been worshippers of the goddess Kāli, the destructive and dark aspect of the Mother Goddess.

Compartmentalization

On an individual level, Indian men and women who are educated and westernized seem to have developed a strategy of compartmentalization to balance the rational and the emotional worlds. While they are rational at work and in their educational, economic and political pursuits, they submit to the irrational religious beliefs and ritual practice without any conflict. In his well-acclaimed study *When a Great Tradition Modernizes: An Anthropological Approach to Indian Civilization* (1972) anthropologist Milton B. Singer observed that an orthodox Brahman can shift back and forth between a highly Western lifestyle at work and very traditional habits at home in all aspects, including language, clothes, food, and ritual practices.

Another way of achieving this balance is to allow women take care of the emotional, religious, and ritual observances. Women and children are believed to have a closer contact with the world of gods and goddesses. Women are also expected to uphold traditions and ensure the continuity of traditional customs through future generations. While in most rural households both women and men may participate in daily observances of rituals, in a city even highly educated men may join in major religious festivals.

Women, even when educated and urbanized, seem to be primarily feminine in the traditional sense and use their academic skill and training to achieve a career without being too deeply influenced by the masculine approach to life. If some of them separate from the traditional values of family and religious belief, they alienate themselves from their cultural and religious roots. However, this state of separation from their cultural archetypes cannot last long without causing neurotic problems. Sometimes aging and life's crises can bring such lost souls back to their gods and goddesses, if not their traditions and customs. If educated Indians argue against their traditions and laugh at age-old customs, they never laugh at their gods and goddesses whose life stories and adventures they grew up listening to and watching in their childhood, at least until very recently.

When intellectual and rational approaches to life's problems do not offer solutions, educated Indians return to the healing divinities again. One Indian woman who left India in her youth to study in an American university embraced Western values and philosophy with the lifestyle for many years. She was successful in her academic work and fairly content with her life free of the constraints of traditional duties and responsibilities. In her advanced years, the alienation from her culture and religion began to be felt through particular neurotic symptoms of total meaninglessness manifested in depression. She then began to dream of the gods and goddesses whom her mother, grandmothers, and great-grandmothers worshipped for generations. In one impressive dream, she had to take out Ziploc plastic bags of frozen figurines of Hindu gods from her freezer and had to thaw them.

In the dream, she knew that she needed to thaw them so she could worship them as her family had done for generations. She knew that this was perhaps the only way she could heal. She was glad that she did not "throw her gods out totally" and that they survived in frozen form. A reestablishment of emotional connection and conscious acknowledgement of her link to her gods made it possible for this woman to return to her cultural archetypes and to find her identity in time and space again. The healing she experienced helped her to reexamine the values of her youth, and she moved to another plane, as it were, to use her education and independence as a woman who went back to her old identity in a new way.

Prolonged Projections

The religious mythology and the life stories of the divine world reflect human existence, and enforce and reinforce social ideals and cultural norms. If mythology is the projection of the collective unconscious, the collective conscious life is strongly influenced by the living experience of the myths through the enactment of everyday rituals. The religious practice works for the individual psyche because the gods and goddesses of the Hindu pantheon are very close to human experience and the worshipper can easily identify and project with the full impact of emotion and fantasies. Such projections can still work because the conscious life and the collective unconscious are not yet separated fully. Perhaps the same mechanism works when the Western youth is carried away by strong identification with a rock musician or the spectators of a movie laugh and cry with the characters on the screen they watch. In India, mass media such as movies attract millions of people every day not only to the fantastic world of unattainable luxury and pleasure, but also the stories about gods and goddesses and divinely powerful women who are ideal wives and mothers. If a number of popular movies today specialize in violence, they usually end with the age-old message of the solidarity of a family, where brothers embrace brothers and husbands reconcile to misunderstood and suffering wives.

C.G. Jung talks about projection, the vitally important psychological process, as follows:

> Projection results from the archaic identity of subject and object, but is properly so called only when the need to dissolve the identity with the object has already risen. This need arises when the identity becomes a disturbing factor, i.e., when the absence of the projected content is a hindrance to adaptation and its withdrawal into the subject has become desirable.[21]

In India for most people, the need for withdrawal of projection from the gods and goddesses has not yet arisen. The real-life situation generally couched in social and cultural reality also allows religious projections to continue because such projections remain highly adaptive.

Once the emotions connected to the numinous and sacred world cease to operate — when the life stories of the divine figures cease to enchant and compel — perhaps then the gods and goddesses will become the subject matter for research, rather than the objects of love, worship, and fear. This condition also precipitates a separation, and a consciousness of suffering follows. The worshippers cease to be healed by the participation of the divine world.

As long as the religious projection continues, the negative aspect of the contrasexual archetype seems unproblematic. Either the negative archetype is projected onto some negative divinity or onto socially accepted relationships. For example, in a society where motherhood is idealized, the cruel mother-in-law is also customary. Part of the negative archetype may even remain unconscious. Only a certain amount of skepticism and questioning knowledge interferes with the projection. I have already described how a group of educated people lose the unquestioned faith, therefore the benefit of the healing impact of projection onto the devine world. I have also mentioned how some of them cope with this loss by a strategy of compartmentalization and how a few may return to the healing archetypes through neurotic sufferings.

Conclusion

In summary, let me reiterate that women in India are more rooted in their feminine archetypes in both positive and negative aspects. The goddesses of the Hindu pantheon are alive in the household shrines that are the private world of worshipping for the women in the family. Most Indian women are also nurtured by their instinctive roles as daughters, wives, and mothers — roles and behaviors strongly supported by social ideals and cultural norms, which in turn are modeled after well-known mythological examples. Thus, the connecting link among her biological, social, cultural, and religious identities is strong. If a woman, by life's circumstances, becomes alienated from this secure identity of the containing feminine culture and religion, psychologically she may not have a choice but to accept the challenge. The animus of such a woman who is usually projected onto her gods may be deprived of the projections and create a restless energy to disturb her psyche. Like the woman mentioned earlier who had to thaw her frozen gods in her dream, through her suffering she may reconnect with her archetypal roots — a process that may transform her to a newer consciousness. This consciousness gives her knowledge about herself without rejecting the irrational side, which brings emotions that heal her neurosis. Thus, a balance between her animus and her femininity can be maintained. However, not many Indian women are facing this possibility yet.

Hindu India, with a religion dominated by a polytheistic pantheon consisting of the goddesses who are closely linked to the lives of humans, offers a different stage for the interplay of the masculine and the feminine archetypes as expressed in the lives of men and women. The struggle and the balance between the sexes find another expression because the psychological atmosphere is predominantly feminine, with both protective and destructive aspects. For better or for worse, women and men in India are contained in the maternal archetype. When the animus, or the masculine mode tries to interfere with either collective or individual life, the balance becomes precarious and the *shakti* of the feminine archetype reestablishes itself through the destructive power of violence, chaos, and death, hopefully to face and defeat the ultimate evil. Goddess Durga did the same by successfully subduing the buffalo demon in the mythology known to all Indians who are reminded and reconnected to the myth by an annual celebration of the ritual for four days. The goddess is thus appeased and adored by the annual worshipping so that the worshippers are protected from calamities. Gods such as Shiva and Krishna are also worshipped by an Indian woman to help her achieve a balance both within and without. They are her animus figures who guide her to remain connected to the feminine archetype personified by the goddess. Thus, Hindu Indians manage not to banish their female goddesses into the depth of the unconscious or archaeological past, at least so far, and women are still in a position to reconnect with them via household or community rituals that heal them.

ENDNOTES

16 Simply put the *Puranas* refer to the Hindu mythology. The literal meaning of the word is "a story of the old days." Written in Sanskrit verses possibly over a period between 300 to 1000 A.D. from oral recollections this encyclopedic book of stories overlaps with the great Indian epic *The Mahabharata*. The *Puranas* have eighteen volumes each attributed to specific gods and their rituals along with other supernatural beings and even tales of ordinary men and women. Many of the stories of the goddess Durga come from the volume called *Devi Purana,* perhaps a later edition to the compendium.

17 Durga also known as Devi and many other names is the most important of the female divinities of the Hindu pantheon. Her life stories are written up in a separate volume of the *Puranas*. She is worshipped in every autumn with great pomp and grandeur as the Mother goddess who holds the power of protection and destruction both. Her popularity and influence go beyond the geographical boundary of India and is worshipped in many countries of Southeast Asia mostly in her benevolent aspect.

18 It is necessary to distinguish between the English word 'power' and the Sanskrit and modern Indian term *shakti*, because the meaning of *shakti* encompasses more than power. *Shakti's* power comes from the archetypal roots therefore transpersonal and not in ego's control. See also Manisha Roy's "The Concept of Femininity and Liberation in the Context of Changing Sex-Roles: Women in Modern India and America" In Dana Raphael (ed) *Being Female: The Hague:* Mouton,1975.

19 The extremely low rate of divorce (1.1%) in India can be explained by several reasons. Apart from the age-old tradition of high value in marriage that is founded in the model of the devine couple of Shiva and Durga, with a rising economy the increasing number of women being the second wage-earner in a marriage, the power struggle within the marriage has shifted. Modern and younger women are reluctant to tolerate spousal abuse (verbal and physical) and are rebelling against the patriarchal family structure. Already there is a tendency of increasing statistics among the millinial married couples of the large cities, divorce among the rural population still nearly nonexistent.

20 Even before Gandhi there were other reformers and scholars like Raja Rammohan Roy, Iswar Chandra Vidyasagar, Rabindranath Tagore, to name a few, who urdently tried to introduce education for women. This trend seemed to have existed also in a few other Asian countried such as Sri Lanka, Burma and Thailand. Men in these countries seem to be less competitive and are willing to encourage women to be educated and become part of work force. These men appreciate the organizing quality of women. In a typical middle-class Indian family it is not uncommon to find the father going against the conservative women folk and encourage the daughters to go for higher education and jobs outside home. During last half a century women have been going out to train for paying jobs for economic reasons alone. See, Manisha Roy's *Bengali Women.*

21 Jung, C.G (1971, '74) "Psychological Types," *Collected Works* vol. 6, paragraph 783.

PART TWO

CHAPTER 3

Individuals and Archetypes

Introduction

This part of the book will concentrate on demonstrating how individual women in American society experience the impact and influence of both feminine and masculine archetypes in their lives from birth to death. This part, therefore, exemplifies some of the generalizations made in the first chapter of Part I on the collective behaviors as lived and experienced by women. In this chapter the individual life stories can capture the emotional experience of the archetypes in a way that the theoretical concepts and ideas are further enlivened by the reality of flesh and blood.

While archetypes dictate and guide human emotions and actions from an invisible depth of the collective unconscious, how an individual reacts and deals with the experience determines the uniqueness of each person's life. When a woman lives a life with an awareness of the archetypal foundation, even the most chaotic or ordinary life takes on additional meaning and significance, as if a purpose toward a goal of fulfilled destiny – whatever that may be –is at work. This explains and justifies apparently meaningless sufferings in life. Life's difficulties and problems seem to move individuals toward a certain expansion of personality, leading toward individuation. However, many people go through life without any such awareness of a process of individuation, although they may attain it through sheer living. In modern times, it appears that conscious realization of life's purpose is extremely helpful to one's emotional security. It helps to know that no matter how insignificant, each person's life is part of a grand scheme of nature's work beyond individual biological existence. Knowledge and experience of archetypes in life can help a human being to move toward transcendence.

Identification, Projection and Integration

Before we look at individual life stories, let me here summarize some of the ways this interplay between the individual ego and the archetypes takes place. Vitally important psychological processes are identification, projection, and assimilation. A child begins its life with the initial identification (participation mystique) with the mother and its surroundings. As it grows older and acquires speech, the child gradually begins to separate its ego from the object of identification. For example, when a child utters the word "I" for the first time rather than using her name in third person as everyone else does, she is aware of an ego of her own. After this major act of separation from the object of identification, the mother, a person throughout her life continues to identify with different people or ideas or images at different times only temporarily and never so totally as in early infancy unless one is psychotic. However, identification at later age can be also very intense for a very brief period.

While identification makes the ego merge fully with the object of identification, in projection, ego remains in its position and only certain unconscious aspects of the personality become projected onto an outer object. For example, when a leader of a nation believes and announces that he *is* the nation, he identifies with the country. His countrymen may project the fatherland or the father-figure on him because their unconscious needs to be led by a father figure are great. Similarly in the act of "falling in love," we project the unacknowledged positive aspect of our animus (or anima) onto the outer person, and the strong emotional and physical attraction pulls us toward the object of projection for a purpose of not only our own individuation but other mysteries as well.

Introjection or assimilation is a process that follows identification and projection, both of which may last only a brief period of time. Ego consciousness seems to demand a movement by withdrawal of projections, which is followed by introjections by the ego of the unconscious contents that were previously projected. Development of a personality and the maturation of a human being must go through these processes of identification, projection, and the eventual withdrawal of both throughout life so that the ego can become more and more conscious by assimilating the unconscious contents as much as possible. All these processes are experienced by the ego through pleasure and pain – identifications and projections beginning with intense pleasure followed by the pain of disillusionment when identification dissolves or projections are withdrawn.

The Christian myth of blissful paradise and its loss symbolizes this very basic psychic reality and, as the myth of Genesis implies, without losing the blissful paradise, humans cannot be conscious. Moreover, it is a snake and a woman who bring the fruit of knowledge that ends the blissful ignorance and brings pain and disillusionment. In the everyday life of each individual, this myth is acted out many times in life, allowing a human being to separate from the identification with and projection of the archetypes to ensure the ego's consciousness.

Two important points to remember about these processes are that, first, they are unconscious and autonomous without ego's knowledge and control, and second, the intense emotional experience of pleasure and pain is part of the process. We are helpless pawns who must project and carry projections despite all our determined intentions and decisions. However, as a person goes through these processes with a certain amount of understanding and acceptance, the consciousness increases to incorporate the unconscious contents into personality (assimilation), and the need for projections and identifications seem to wane. Religions such as Hinduism and Buddhism describe the ultimate state of this gradually expanded consciousness as *moksha* or *nirvana*. While every human being must go through these processes of pleasure and pain, the emotional reaction to these unconscious and autonomous processes may vary from person to person depending on the sensitivity of the individual personality and the ego's strength.

The autonomous power of projection and its withdrawal are most intensely felt in human love and best described by novelists and poets. Consider the following example in the classic novel *Of Human Bondage* by W. Somerset Maugham, where the hero's feelings as a lover are expressed:

> "For a moment he remembered all the anguish he had suffered on her account, and he was sick with the recollection of his pain. But, it was no more than recollection. When he looked at her he knew he no longer loved her. ... He was surprised that the old feeling had left him so completely. ... Suddenly his heart gave a sort of twist in his body; He saw a woman in front of him who he thought was Mildred, and then when the woman turned, he saw it was someone unknown to him. ... He was infinitely relieved, but it was not only relief that he felt; it was disappointment too; ... That love had caused him so much suffering that he knew he would never, never quite be free of it. Only death could assuage his desire." [22]

Another example of such heart-rending pain after the love-projection is withdrawn is found in the words of Queen Orual over her lost love in C.S. Lewis's novel *Till We Have Faces: A Myth Retold*:

> "But when the craving went, nearly all that I called myself went with it. It was as if my whole soul had been one tooth and now the tooth was drawn. I was a gap. And now I thought I had come to the very bottom and that the gods could tell me no worse." [23]

While both the experiences of projection and its withdrawal can be equally pleasurable and painful, as can be glimpsed in these quotations, the vital importance of its experience is well-expressed by C.G. Jung in the following:

> If the soul-image is not projected, a thoroughly morbid relation to the unconscious gradually develops. The subject is increasingly overwhelmed by unconscious contents, which his inadequate relation to the object makes him powerless to assimilate or put to any kind of use, so that the whole subject-object relation only deteriorates further. [24]

We saw how collective projections of archetypal figures and rituals honoring them can form a psychologically healing atmosphere in the lives of Hindu Indians. In the case of Western experience, such projections seem to have become a hindrance to adaptation and were withdrawn to make room for the development of consciousness and for newer kinds of projections as well. Similar processes seem to take place in the individual psyche, and today, many of the archetypal needs are awaiting newer forms of projection on both the collective and personal levels. For example, in the institution of marriage, the form and shape have undergone considerable changes during last three or four decades. Some of these changed forms may eventually become institutionalized, finding support in the legal and socio-economic systems.

What are the implications of all these changes in institutional forms for an individual? In a woman's life, her femininity and her animus both must find expression and development through her psychological evolution – through identification, projection, and, hopefully, assimilation of some of the attributes. For a modern American woman, her animus seems to be the vital agent in this process of assimilation. Both her repressed feminine shadow – something her cultural role rejects – and the animus in many forms are identified with and/or projected onto outer objects during various phases of a woman's life. By creating disturbing sensations, the animus initiates the separation of the ego from the projected object for further psychological development. This can happen as a new human figure or as a new idea that stirs a woman from her comfortable projection. The dramatic symbolic expression of the agent creating the separation of the feminine ego from her identification with the mother archetype is in the abduction and rape of Persephone by Hades, the king of the underworld in Greek mythology.

The lives of women I propose to follow through various stages to see how they experience the archetypes come from my anthropological fieldwork and analytic practice. I changed the names, places, and some facts of their lives for obvious reasons of confidentiality and privacy.

Childhood and Adolescence

Joyce

I propose to begin with a stereotypical middle-class, white, Anglo-Saxon American family, headed by a father in his 40s, who was a consultant in a large industrial company. Both he and his wife had college educations, and had parents with college educations, but are not actively religious, although they nominally professed to be Protestant. The father earned enough to provide the family with a comfortable home with all the latest gadgets in the kitchen, a couple of holidays each year, and even private schooling for the two children. Apart from the usual two cars and other household amenities, the family had several credit cards and less than a thousand dollars in a savings account. The year was 1975. The daughter (whom I shall call Joyce) was 14 when I first got to know the family. She was the younger of the two siblings; her brother was 17 at that time and was finishing high school. Her mother was 42, fairly attractive, extroverted, and pleasant.

Joyce was brought up with an enormous number of toys, most of which were mechanical. Her toys included mostly feminine things, but also a few boys' toys, such as balls and a few small cars. The mother was already interested in giving the daughter more of a gender-neutral upbringing than she herself had received. I found the mother widely read in child psychology and included popular psychological jargon in her everyday conversation. She took pride in being aware of the changes that had been happening around her. She and her women friends of a similar age and background with similarly busy husbands spent a lot of time discussing these issues and were open to any new experiments in their children's upbringing.

I found the mother intelligent and well-informed in many things that were provided by the media and friends. She seemed to nurture some "notions" and "ideas" about things in life and was guided by them. Her talks with me were often discussions and views either in accordance with or against certain social or political situations. Only rarely would she indulge in speaking about something personal and emotional. I found her tiring often. Her daughter, on the other hand, seemed more direct with her emotional reactions to situations and things when we were alone. However, she, too, began to be influenced by some vague "ideas," which were not too different from those of her mother's. She confessed that most of the time she was confused about her future and who she really was.

A typical family interaction took place around the dinner table with all four members of the family present. Food was ordinary and geared to satisfy all four to some extent: a particular type of beef for the husband, potatoes for the son and Coca-Cola for Joyce. The mother neither enjoyed nor disliked cooking. Small talks over dinner ranged from little household matters to plans for a weekend outing or a party. Sometimes, the father had to swallow a few complaints regarding an unfixed faucet in the bathroom or some other oversight. He usually responded with a few mild jokes to brush aside such routine allegations or would promise to do it the very next day and change the topic by mentioning a neighbor, which led the couple to a gossipy mood. The brother hardly talked and often brought a book to the table. Sometimes both parents would object to this; sometimes they would ignore it completely. They finished eating rather quickly to get back to their individual evenings – father to the television, mother to her phone calls and a bit of television, and the children to their individual rooms to do homework or whatever they wanted.

Both children had their own television sets, along with their own stereos and records. The number of records exceeded the number of books on both children's shelves. During the week, it was the mother who did most of the errands around the house and with the children. She made the doctor's appointments, drove them to their schools or playgrounds, and attended parent-teacher meetings most of the time. The father was informed if there was a bigger-than-usual crisis in the family. Over the weekends, the father and the son played or watched football or baseball together at least once and did some repairs around the house or on the cars. Joyce felt that her brother had a lot more contact with her father than she did after she turned 9 or 10.

She recalled how her father had taken her for short walks sometimes on Saturday mornings to the nearby drugstore to pick up *The New York Times* and he would buy a special kind of candy that she loved. This was a secret between them; they were not supposed to tell the mother or the brother about this "unhealthy" sticky indulgence. Although she was small then and hardly came up to her father's thigh, she had felt closer to him then than she feels now. She could not remember why things had changed. Suddenly, she had lost contact with him and, since that time, had had no idea how to break the ice. They had become strangers. Occasionally, they would have some exchanges at the dinner table, but a tension remained. Her mother, on the other hand, became closer to her during her teens (they went shopping together a lot), although recently there seemed to be a kind of tension between them as well.

All this puzzled Joyce very much. Once, she told me that her gradually cooling relationship with her father must have something to do with the relationship between her parents, but she could not be sure how. Sometimes she felt as if she had committed something mysteriously wrong in the eyes of her parents. As far as her brother was concerned, Joyce had little to say. To her, he was immature, ill-mannered, and uninteresting. His friends were even worse. They talked about baseball or football and chased dumb girls. She spent more and more time with her girlfriends partly because it was not much fun being at home. Her friends, too, bored her at times, talking constantly about clothes and boys and "dates." She realized she could not always be involved in such superficialities, yet she had little choice if she wanted to be included, and gradually she began to feel more like one of them. Her identity crisis seemed more confused than critical, and her talks often brought that to the forefront.

Comments

Although Joyce was growing up in the late 1970s and early 1980s, her case is quite representative of the difficulties and usual lifestyle a middle-class white American girl experiences perhaps even today, at least in the following aspects. If her childhood begins with a demonstrative closeness to her father in a fairy-tale way, it is cut off by the time she is in her mid-teens. In most Western urban families, an alliance seems to establish itself along sexual lines, despite the fact that there is little outward segregation, as in older cultures. The emotional connection between the brother and sister is also often fraught with competition and distance. This is interesting, especially in view of the fairly "masculine" atmosphere that a girl is brought up in. She is given similar values as her brother as far as the need to make good grades. Her school curricula are quite similar to her brother's, and she is encouraged to do well, at least through high school. She learns to expect similar material and mechanized comforts when she is young and as she grows up.

When Joyce was growing up (in the early 1980s), most high school girls had even begun to play so-called boys' sports such as soccer, hockey, and some baseball. This was part of the effect of the feminist movement that became strongly vocal during the late 1960s, demanding equality on as many levels as possible. The message from the women's movement that a girl could be as good as her brother or even better was loud and clear. She also does well in sports, especially because the need to compete and succeed in sports and bodybuilding is already inculcated in both sexes. In the development of both intellect (academic) and physical fitness, her identification with the animus was important at this period of her life.

The first sprouting of the animus in the projections of the girl within her family seems absolutely vital to determine her later development, both in the archetypal sense and in outer relationships with the opposite sex. After the very unconscious identification with the mother, her projection onto the father is critical for her gradual separation from the identification with her mother. Seeds of the future erotic relationship with her animus, both inner and outer, are planted at this time, and a few years later she goes through a phase of both identification and projection together, when she may live out the phase of a tomboy.

Tomboy Phase

During this phase, a girl can behave like a boy, playing boys' games, climbing trees, and indulging in boyish mischief. She may become quite competitive in these activities and may even achieve a high position in the eyes of other boys, although some bullies may treat her as a lesser being. Her companionship with boys who treat her just like another boy gives her a satisfaction and an excitement that she seems to need just before puberty. In a lecture given by Adolf Guggenbühl-Craig, a Swiss Jungian analyst of Zurich, it was mentioned that the latency period of adolescence does not seem to have any mentionable mythological parallel, at least in Greek mythology. However, in most old societies (and even in Western societies a generation or two ago), girls (if they were not married as child brides) were allowed to live this social archetypal role before they flipped over to the other roles of shy and demure girls in need of sexual protection from boys they played with only yesterday. A beautiful example of this is given by Jane H. Wheelwright in a published lecture titled "Women and Men"; her own adolescence on a Western cattle ranch is told as follows:

> As a child and teenager I was expected to compete with my brothers in riding, roping, hunting and climbing trees, to take physical risks of all kinds, and to bear the same respon-sibilities as they. ... Far from resenting all this, my brothers were proud of me and boasted to their friends of my physical strength and prowess! Furthermore, their attitude of approval and acceptance of me as a person was shared by all the men I encountered in our wilderness area. Recognizing that I carried my own weight, they welcomed me as a bona fide member of the ranching operation. This approbation by the males in my environment made it unnecessary for me to feel competitive with them.[25]

In India, even in villages and towns where girls are sometimes not married until their late teens and early 20s, they participate in boys' games and activities. There are neighborhood organizations and clubs that recruit both boys and girls, and their participation requires a fair amount of physical activity and sports. It is possible that a certain amount of sex segregation is a necessary precondition for this tendency to be allowed by the society. In the modern West, a girl experiences the masculine world early in most of her roles as a girl, which overlap with those of boys.

A girl in her tomboy phase uses her body actively, as if only to prepare for a quieter and more introverted phase with the onset of menstruation. This physical expression that a young girl's animus is allowed to find in collaboration with boys in her pre-puberty years may be more vital for her later physical and mental health than we know. Sonja Marjasch, a Swiss Jungian analyst/therapist, talks about some of her women patients — women in their 30s — who sometimes demonstrate the animus problem through a stiff rigidity of their bodies. Their body language may convey their neuroses better than their dreams. The therapist's suggestions of physical activity such as dancing, swimming, riding, or running to some of her most difficult cases helped increase their self-confidence and seemed to enable them to take a better stand in regard to their psychological problems. Body therapy and even something like highly rigorous training such as the martial arts can provide deeply satisfying emotional experiences for some women.[26]

However, girls do not always have opportunities to live out their competitive aggressive aspects in formal ways. Sports, especially competitive ones, offer such an opportunity. One need only watch great female figures in the Olympic Games to realize how blessed by their contrasexual archetypes they must be, to reach such summits of success in so-called masculine sports. Perhaps the significant point here is the necessity of taming and disciplining the talent to a creative pleasure. Without the disciplined training, all archetypal talents remain primitive and impersonal. Their humanization and transformation seem to need the ego's determination to deal with the situation as a duty to obey their contrasexual needs. The expression of such needs and talents requires hard work and training under expert guidance. Schools and camps are appropriate institutions for helping girls of this age to realize the vital need for the development of the animus both in intellect and physical activities.

Such adolescent animus needs through physical sports and activity are important to live out before the onset of puberty — a traumatic physical and psychological change for a girl. Is it possible that the animus of this stage, if remains unlived, may go underground only to manifest itself later perhaps in psychosomatic discomforts or even illnesses? Indeed, unlived phases of the animus development may continue to create neurotic problems, and sometimes a grown woman has to go back to the earlier experience psychologically.

A 32-year-old Swiss woman client of mine lived in another country as a child and played with boys climbing trees and doing other boyish activities. She had to return to a restricted Swiss convent atmosphere before she was 12, cutting short her tomboy phase. In her 30s, she had recurrent dreams in which she climbed trees and scaled walls of gardens. Climbing a tree had become a healing symbol in her dream life. Ideally, the tomboy phase should be preceded and followed by the girl's identification with her own feminine archetype, if the stages of her development are viewed as a natural movement for balance between her feminine self and her animus.

A child of an enlightened modern mother who tried to minimize the double standard of a girl's and a boy's upbringing, Joyce never became too much of a girl even as a child. She played with fewer dolls than toy cars. Her mother had not been secure in her own feminine identity to let her instincts guide her in bringing up the daughter. The mother was brought up to be a dutiful and efficient wife and mother. Another mother in her 50s who is a lot more aware than Joyce's mother told me: "An American mother is brought up to be a good mother by suppressing her spontaneous instinctual side if these feelings are negative, such as anger. She is also not supposed to be depressed or introverted. She must always nurture her family with a smile and without any sign of frustrations." One way to achieve this is to be guided by one's rational thinking alone. Joyce's mother was so practiced in this way of playing her role as a mother that she did not even know that she lost her own feminine instinct somewhere along the way. To cover this loss, she equipped herself with well-educated opinions, which gave her the illusion of knowledge and understanding.

She was as puzzled as her husband over matters of the heart and soul, and it was only natural that her daughter sought her feminine peers for advice the mother could not offer.

In addition to this very unfeminine atmosphere, Joyce also lacked a healthy relationship with the two males in her family. The relationship with her brother was indifferent because they shared similar education and ideas. There was not enough opposition between her and her brother's worlds to encourage her to view him as a healthy competition or a complement to herself. She did not have an opportunity to learn to live and deal with a male counterpart who was not just a sex partner. This lack in her upbringing has serious implications in terms of her inner relationship with her animus. Her contrasexual archetype could not be lived through projection on her brother or father.

Puberty

When Joyce was faced with her puberty one day, this was less of an event than her obtaining the driver's license, which marked an adult state by giving her the freedom to drive a car on her own. Neither her mother nor her education or her peers had prepared her, despite all the equality she enjoyed with her brother. After all, she was different from the boys in one very significant way. Joyce's mother, as expected and like most American mothers of her time, took a very clinical and enlightened approach to the daughter's onset of menstruation. As I visited them soon after this event, I remember how casually they treated the whole issue.

I found out about it only because the mother told me how she was proud of being a helpful mother by giving her daughter the best practical advice for the safest contraceptives. This clinical approach allowed no mystery or trauma to linger, and both mother and daughter took the situation in a matter-of-fact way. By dealing with the necessary nuisance of cramps by taking a couple of aspirins, they felt they had overcome the anatomical destiny. Mothers who are not as enlightened may help their daughters acquire a lifelong disgust for a "curse," which for some unknown reason women are born to suffer.

Several authors, both women and men, have explored the impact of menstruation on the growing identity of an adolescent girl.[27] In older societies and cultures that are technologically primitive, a girl is prepared for adult life right at the onset of menstruation to realize that her sexuality and body are vitally important, not only for her to become a mother to create other human beings, but more importantly, to feel as a tiny part of the bigger numinous power of the creative feminine archetype operating through her. This sense of connection with the eternal and creative feminine remains with her throughout her life, continuously reinforced through her sexual and instinctive roles.

For example, in northeast India, a girl at her first menstruation goes through a ceremony called the "little wedding." She is married symbolically to a natural object, a plant or an animal, perhaps to establish her eternal connection with the Nature, the original and the ultimate feminine archetype. The ritual not only connects her with Mother Nature and the sacred world of the supernatural but also offers her a link to her community and society. The tremendous import of the event, not only for venerating her sexuality but also for the sake of the society and her culture, is emphasized by such a ritual.

Using a matter-of-fact attitude toward her first menstruation, which can be regulated by pills and ignored by physical activities, a young woman loses the above-mentioned connection with the numinous feminine archetype forever. Part of the reason the awesome significance of the first menstruation is reduced is that the possibility of pregnancy is now controllable by the easy availability of contraceptives. All this, which resulted from an increasing development of a masculine and rational consciousness, pushes the adolescent girl into an identity crisis that is not too different from that of her male counterpart. Erik Erikson describes this identity confusion as the paramount problem of today's youth, and their means of solution take the form of what he calls a "false ideology"[28] to which they turn to avoid confusion. In extreme cases the teenagers often turn to pop music and even drugs

Sexuality - Awakening

Perhaps an identification with the animus takes place here for some girls, while for others, turning to their sexuality becomes another solution. The obsession of teenage girls in most high schools in America with finding sexual experience as soon and as frequently as possible appears similar to the obsessive needs for sexual conquests of adolescent boys. I suspect the animus is acting like a teenage boy who must have numerous sexual encounters to prove his masculinity. The superficiality that Joyce complained of in her girlfriends who constantly seek dates and sexual contacts attests to this obsessive drive.

A theologian and psychologist, Penelope Washburn, writes:

> A young woman often turns to her sexuality to protect her from the implications of this identity crisis. She defines herself in terms of her attractiveness to boys and focuses all value in her need to be loved. ... Her sexuality is manipulative since it is expressed, not from self-love, but out of a desperate need to find identity in being loved. ... This type of solution is socially condoned and reinforced by advertising and the media. It is destructive because it fails to recognize that personal identity cannot be given by others.[29]

The change in sexual mores and the easy availability of contraceptives in last half of the past century not only in America but also in Europe and some other parts of the world have released a girl of 15 today from apprehension and anxiety about her sexual encounters. Even her mother offers her the practical instructions on preventing pregnancy. Her mother and she both feel that they have control over the situation and can determine and indulge in their sexual adventures. This realization of control is not without a certain amount of independence and positive reliance on oneself, if one's instinctive judgment remains intact.

The lack of contact with the male members of her family just before and after puberty may create the strong identification with the animus-like expression of such activities. That is, the necessary projections that a girl before puberty needs to have on her male family members are lived. And the animus remains in the unconscious, only to be lived through identification with some of the traits that appear alien and even destructive to the feminine psyche.

The excessive and obsessive quality of sexual adventures that modern middle and high school girls in America seem free to indulge in may also have something to do with the need to contact the numinosity that has been more of a transpersonal archetypal need and looms in the depths of the unconscious. The widespread use of contraceptives freed adolescent girls from the fear of pregnancy, as well as the traumatic ambivalence associated with the first sexual experience without love.

During the early part of my analytic practice in the 1980s, all my women patients from America, England, and Switzerland between the ages of 25 and 40 could not remember anything special about their first sexual encounter. Only those who had incestuous relations by force reported a traumatic experience, if it hadn't been repressed. In the early part of 1980s, I decided to find out if my sample was really biased. Two hundred random and anonymous responses from different parts of America to my questionnaire by mail corroborated the previous findings. Some women even asked why this information was at all important. These 200 women were between 20 and 50 years of age.

Erich Neumann, in his sensitive work on the psychological stages of feminine development, presents the significance of this experience with the archetypal masculine.[30] According to Neumann, the childhood and adolescence of a girl (in earlier times) was strictly protected by the female group, which conserved itself with the help of a separation from the masculine world, sometimes in antagonism against it. The encounter of the young post-pubescent girl and a young man happened through an invasion of the masculine archetype — a numinous experience that may not even be connected to a human male directly. It was often experienced as a formless masculine power, a ravishing archetypal penetration symbolized in Greek mythology by the rape of Persephone.

A young woman may dream of animals chasing her. This overpowering penetration may be as devastating as the sexual rape of a young girl by an unknown figure, and she must surrender. Through this surrender, as Neumann sees it and I agree, she experiences her deep feminine nature, although the contact is with the impersonal masculine archetype. Paradoxically, this phallic encounter seems necessary before she can separate herself from her identification with the feminine world so that she can be connected more consciously and deeply to it.

Formal marriage to a human male is only a concrete expression of this phallic encounter. Her husband frees her from the imprisonment in the feminine world at this time. Later, much later, when she is old, she may go back to reconnect to her feminine spirituality on another level. This process, Neumann adds, rarely runs smoothly in a woman's development, and she may be stuck or fixated in one stage or another, precipitating neurotic suffering at its worst. Usually such difficulties are expressed through a lifelong father complex with its underlying compulsion and aura that are associated with the archetype of the animus.

While Neumann's scheme seems to apply well to a fairly undisturbed feminine world that may bring a girl up to maturity, today's situation in America, as described so far, seems quite a bit different. At least outwardly, a girl is not being nurtured in such a homogeneously protective feminine atmosphere anymore. As we have noticed already, a modern girl's initial identification with the feminine world is no longer strong and deep enough to make the masculine penetration a traumatic necessity. By repeating the sexual experience, she does not achieve any deeper connection to herself or to her masculine archetype but is left with a jaded and worn-out feeling, sometimes before she even reaches the age of 30. Such experiences may often lead to sexual frigidity, or a driven quality in sexual activity remains a lifelong pattern. In either case, these women remain psychological virgins despite many sexual contacts, marriages, or even motherhood. One striking dream of an American woman of 30 shows the psychological image of Neumann's contention beautifully.

She comes from an upper-middle-class, educated family with a cold mother and a strong, ambivalent relationship to the father. She was married and divorced, has a 2-year-old child, and had numerous love affairs both during and after the marriage. The following dream has been a recurrent one that she dreamed nearly for two years twice every month until she came to analysis.

> A girlfriend and I were kidnapped by a gang of hoodlums who tied us up and raped us by inserting broken glass bottles into our vaginas. My girlfriend bled to death, and I somehow crawled to a telephone booth to call for help and succeeded in getting help. I was badly injured.

Her comments written after the dream were:

> I felt horrible every time I had this nightmare, yet I also felt a sense of catharsis when I woke up. This horrible dream seemed to have done something for me. Surprisingly enough, my sex-life became a deeper experience.

This woman also had a couple of dreams where bulls or other big animals with threatening horns were chasing her.

For a modern woman who cannot experience the numinous penetration of the masculine archetype in her first sexual encounter, it may come through as a nightmare like this, where the horror of rape replaces the trauma of the numinous. In this regard, her emotional reaction to the dream is illuminating and quite in accordance with the point Neumann makes. One wonders if the increasing occurrence of physical rape in many cities of America may not point to a terrifying archetypal reality that the masculine must achieve the contact with the feminine through sexual violence on a mass scale. The trauma of the first contact is thus imposed through violence. Similar speculations can be made about the fascination and attraction for the danger and risk involved in the drug world. A young woman (or man) must visit the underworld of death and danger through this means alone. The need for the abduction and rape of Hades may still remain in the psyche of modern Persephones.

Adolescence and Mental Health

The neurotic manifestations of the disturbances in the development of the growing animus in a woman's adolescence can take many shapes and forms, depending on the individual's relationships with her mother and father. The mother's relationship with her own animus, as well as with the husband, and the father's relationship with his anima and his wife are important factors. In other words, a girl's unconscious relationships to her feminine and masculine archetypes are vital in creating an imbalance that may be quite unhealthy. The complexity of many little-known and unknown conditions influencing the personality of a young woman is perhaps most poignantly exemplified by anorexia.

A psychosomatic problem that can even lead to death, anorexia attacks mostly girls in their teens and women in their early 20s. The increasing incidence of this disease in recent decades in both America and West European countries has led many psychiatrists, psychologists, and researchers to pay greater attention to the genesis and morphology of this illness. According to many, a distant and cold relationship with the father during the critical years of a girl's puberty, along with an unfeminine (or perhaps too feminine) mother may be the cause. The anorexic girl's denial of her developing body and budding womanhood and her complex relationship to food indicate a combination of both masculine and feminine archetypal problems. In today's world, for a young woman to prepare herself for a future, a balance between maternal security and a healthy relationship to the father is essential. Pressure for outward independence may be threatening before she has separated from her identification with the mother fully. At any rate, the absence of emotional contact with the father and the archetypal father may damage the normal development of a woman's animus. However, a lot more research and observations are needed before we can even begin to understand the complex psychosomatic illnesses like anorexia and bulimia.

I cannot avoid mentioning that the other glaring problem teenagers and some adults face is addiction. Volumes have been written and discussed about this extremely troubling issue. I only have space to mention briefly one aspect of this hugely important topic. Addiction with any kind of substance abuse seems to be a failed attempt to compensate for the lack of meaningful spiritual elements in a modern teenager's life. In other words, addiction may lure a teenage girl or boy to get in touch with the dark aspect of the deeper Self. It is an archetypal onslaught that has to be faced and handled with discipline, care, and guidance. Oftentimes the girls or boys lack such caring guidance, unfortunately.

Without the benefit of a strong puberty ritual supported by the cultural tradition as in many ancient and tribal societies, the girls and boys are more confused than ever and desperately try to grow up. Addiction is a tempting option that helps them sidestep the sudden responsibility of growing up. This observation is only one of the possible explanations of the epidemic proportion of addictive behavior among the adolescents and adults. Death from drug addiction among present-day American youths is a severe social problem that is being handled by the politicians and mental health professionals without understanding the deeper issues. The current statistics of over 100 deaths a day (some of them may be above teenage) from the opioid overdose in several cities of America is a calamity of great concerns at the time of writing this book.

Connected to addictive behavior, another kind of problem may begin at this time and may accompany a woman all her life, and may be described as various manifestations of the archetype "puella," the "eternal girl." A puella is a woman who finds it extremely hard to relate to her own masculine side as well as to men. The connection with the animus seems to have been damaged severely, perhaps for generations. As a result, she appears to be tied up in an undeveloped femininity without the balance of the opposite. In her book *The Wounded Woman* (1982), Linda Leonard explores the various patterns of the "puella" existence in a woman's life.[31] She describes several archetypal patterns a woman's psychological adaptation may result from a maladjusted relationship with the father, a "puer" who himself has not developed into a mature male.

Formal Education

Before leaving the topic of childhood and adolescence of a girl, something must be said about the education system, since nearly all girls today are formally educated at least between the ages of 5 and 18. Earlier I discussed the vital need of disciplining and channeling the animus through regulated exercise and sports. A formal education system allows such opportunities for the intellect and intelligence to be trained, brushed, polished, and enhanced in both boys and girls. Ideally, education should also prepare both boys and girls to learn the skills to apply to real problems of life and qualify them for jobs in order to earn a living. Many girls may go in for practical training after the first 12 years of schooling, and a few go on to university for further academic degrees. Business and nursing schools used to train young women to become secretaries, bookkeepers, and nurses, thereby enabling them to find jobs easily after their training, and perhaps, before their marriage. Now, that picture has totally changed. A woman now goes for any branch of education and training to prepare for the same job a man also can access, including even all branches of the military. But not all Western countries are on the same page in this evolution.

Today many girls go for training to work in commercial firms and industries as secretarial help, technicians, or administrators. Often they stop working after they marry. In America and England or in Scandinavia and Eastern European countries, women need to work to help their husbands to pay the bills or to make their own livings. In other words, more and more women are being trained in skilled professions, and the education girls receive either during the first 12 years or for training toward professional skills are in no way different from that of their brothers. Statistics in American school systems show that girls on the primary school level do better than boys, but may perform poorly as they go on to higher grades.

I wonder if the phenomenon of poor achievement by girls beyond the primary and middle school levels may not have to do with the lack of encouragements from the elders and also the style and quality of education among other factors. A girl finds little to nurture her feminine values and instincts in schools. Her interest in going to school every day may be more due to the prospect of meeting her peers rather than the exciting stimulation in class. Even in a system where girls learn about domestic work, the way such subjects are taught seems to take the creative and imaginative flair out of them.

This problem of rigidity and a confusing but pervasive impact of technology in every aspect of housework lacking creativity and imagination are expressed vividly by the following dream of a 50-year-old woman, who is also suffering from some nagging psychosomatic symptoms. She dreamed:

> I see a violin box in my kitchen. I am surprised and open it to find a computer inside. The computer has various shelves and slots like a vending machine from which prepared food can come out...

The influence of women's movements changed some of the career choices for both genders. Already in the '80s, we saw a trend of increasing number of women joining the military right after the high school for the ostensible purpose of making a better living. Although the conscious reason for such a career choice is economic, the archetypal background of the attraction for the so-called masculine professions fraught with danger cannot be denied. The new trend took some young men to train in so-called feminine professions like nursing, dancing, etc., though the number remained low. One exception was the careers connected to the ever-exploding multibillion-dollar food industry. Men and women alike went to newly established culinary institutes all over the country to be trained as chefs for exponentially increasing numbers of hotels and restaurants. Chefs of both genders could have creative and fulfilling lives, as if they realized their opposites in creating new recipes – an endeavor that incorporates both the science of chemistry and arts of organization, aesthetics, and caring. But this is a fairly recent trend. Women going to the military, including the navy and war journalism, began even earlier.

Girls who show a special interest and ability in science subjects and abstract thinking end up going to universities and in some cases even do extremely well. While they reap satisfaction from obtaining advanced degrees and an opportunity to join professions promising independence and respect, they also have to pay a high price in terms of their femininity. In high school, they learn to adapt to the rational, masculine attitude and a way of thinking that culminates at university, and their need for the development of the feminine side continues to be starved. In my own experience as a university student at several different campuses in two continents and later as a professor at universities in America and West Europe, I have always felt an aridity surrounding women students. Intelligence and brilliance in academic work seem to be inversely proportionate to humor and playfulness. At university or in the professional world of the West, a woman finds her "femininity" more a hindrance than an asset. In a book titled *Women on Top* (1979), Jean Adams writes that many successful professional women she interviewed complained about the constant struggle they faced to keep their feminine values along with their professional aspirations. What made them feminine were antithetical to the efficient dealings in the professional world. Fifteen years later similar statements are made by Maureen Murdock in her book *The Hero's Daughter* (1994) and I quote, "In my ten years of working in Silicon Valley, I have not met one woman who feels good about herself and hasn't abdicated her femininity..." (The full quote is earlier in this book on page 31.)

Emily

Emily, a 48-year-old woman, expressed the above problem well in the following confession:

> When I went to school after the kindergarten, my first test showed such high scores that my parents were extremely proud of me and encouraged me to do well in all subjects. I was quite good in science and mathematics and not so good in social sciences. I was brought up with a feeling of healthy competition

with my brother whose grades at school were not as good as mine. Neither my mother nor I paid much attention to clothes and fashion even when I was in high school. When I went to college, suddenly I discovered that good grades were not enough to attract attention from young men. My classmates talked for hours about fashion, make-ups and boys, and even my mother began to put pressure on me in this respect. I must admit, I was not sure what my real goals were. I knew I had to go along with the crowd and learn to dress and behave more like a college co-ed as the time and era dictated. Otherwise I was afraid I might never be married. On the other hand, I also had fantasies of becoming a scientist someday and perhaps, be famous and well-known.

In the midst of this confused stage, I met my future husband, who showed interest in my intelligent mind and my seriousness toward life. After two years of "going together," we got married. He finished his Master's and I had one more year to go. I continued studying, but soon it seemed impossible to concentrate in studies, and despite my careful precautions, I became pregnant. Since then I have had four children in twelve years, and now that the youngest is beginning college I have time to breathe. So much has happened during these years of my marriage that is not even clear to me. Suddenly I feel cheated, cheated because I never developed my academic talents, and now that children are grown and do not need me I have nothing left.

My husband, who was never too demonstrative, seemed to have drifted away from me slowly. We have little in common any more except the children and their problems. We keep discussing them because we have nothing else to say to each other. I know he had to work hard to support a large family and put the children through college, etc., but I cannot help feeling as if I had the lion's share of sacrifice in bringing up the family. Yet, when we met I was the brighter one and he even acknowledged that. Now, if I want to go back to the university and finish my degrees, I am not even sure I could catch up. Things move so fast in sciences. Sometimes, I feel as if someone somewhere stole my life. I failed somewhere despite all the good grades I got in school and college. I am neither a satisfied wife and mother nor an independent

> successful scientist. Above all, I am very resentful and angry.
> What has my education done to me, except perhaps in making
> me aware that I am a failure?

This rather touching confession by Emily, a woman of 48, when I was doing anthropological field work in 1971, illustrates more than the problem of formal education in a married woman's life. Even if we put aside the obvious facts of her time (her daughters may have more of a choice to use their education than she did), the important question I raised earlier still remains. Not only women but perhaps many men feel similarly with regard to their education and their later work and life. What purpose does then a formal education serve for a girl?

I suggest that, like her tomboy phase, when a young girl identified with the physically active animus, in her school and college years she identified with her intellectually active animus. Whether the present education system allows for the full blossoming of the animus or not is another question. After spending many years of my life in higher education, looking back, I see another aspect of it that I did not see as a student and a young teacher. Now I see the value of formal education not so much for its content but more in training and enriching a young woman's mind. As she benefits physically from sports, she also develops her thinking function and intellectual gift through rigor and discipline. The intellectual aspect of her contrasexual archetype thus becomes trained and developed to be used for herself and in the world, which today is dictated mostly by the same archetype.

ENDNOTES

22   Maugham, W. Somerset (1963, First publ.1915) *Of Human Bondage*, London/New York: Penguin, pp.444, 447, 605.

23   Lewis, C.S. (1956) *Till We have Faces: A Myth Retold*, London/ New York: Harcourt Brace J., page 267.

24   Jung, C.G (1971 and '74), "Psychological Types," *Collected Works*, vol 6, paragraph 811.

25   Wheelwright, Jane H.(1978), *Women and Men*, San Francisco: C.G. Jung Institute of San Francisco Publication. Also see Margaret Mead's *Male and Female* (1969, New York: Dell Pub) for a vivid description of American families with class and ethnic variations.

26   Marjasch, Sonja, "Educating the Animus" A lecture given in London in October, 1963.

27   See for example, Penelope Washbuurn (1977) *Becoming Woman: The Quest for Wholeness in Female Experience*, New York: Harper & Row, pp 26-27; Erich Neumann (1959) "Psychologica Stages of Feminine Development"(Tr. by Rebecca Jacobson) New York: Spring, pp. 63 - 97; Linda Leonard (1978) , "The Puella Patterns" In Psychological Perspectives, vol.9, No. 2

28   Erik H. Erikson in his book *Identity: Youth and Crisis*,(New York: W.W. Norton & Co. 1968, '94) discusses the various steps of positive and negative aspects of the development of a Western youth's identity, which is not so different from those of his sister at this point of time.

29   Washbourn, Penelope, (1977) *Becoming Woman: The Quest for Wholeness in Female Experience*, New York: Harper & Row pp. 26-27.

30   Neumann, Erich (1959) "Psychological Stages Of Feminine Development" (Tr. by Rebecca Jacobson), New York: Spring

31   Leonard, Linda (1982) *The Wounded Woman*, Athens (Ohio): The Swallow Press.

CHAPTER 4

Adult Life

Many Choices, More Confusions

I ended the last chapter by quoting an American woman in her late 40s lamenting the futility of her college education in view of her life as a housewife, wife, and mother for over 20 years after her marriage. In analytical work, we meet women of her generation and some who are younger. Her daughter, who is now beginning college, or who is a teenager, may have more choices than her mother or her grandmother did, unless they were exceptional women. For example, the famous anthropologist Margaret Mead was born at the turn of the 20th century into a family of two generations of academically trained women.

The generation gap between mothers and daughters during the last 50 or even 30 years since the Second World and Vietnam Wars is enormous. I already touched on this issue in the first part of the book. Many factors, including the rapid growth of economy aided by a technological revolution along with an increased aspiration for material comforts, have been at work for quite a while. Unprecedented changes in sexual and religious mores resulted from wide use of contraceptives, legalized abortion and other reproductive innovations, and improved means of communication across the globe have been pushing women toward a new self-consciousness as well as confusion. The resentment and anger that the woman I quoted above felt, are shared by many others, if not for similar reasons. In a rapidly changing lifestyle based on ever-improving and easily accessible technology, the confusion of messages are increased in later lives even more. Men who went ahead in their academic work and earned high positions and felt satisfied with their achievements also began to feel "cheated" somewhere along the line and came to therapy because they felt misunderstood by their wives and other women, and were challenged to face their own femininity, which had been neglected for generations before them. Many of these men thrived in their powerful positions at workplace but had no clue how to handle the power without abusing it as in sexual exploitations of female employees. (I touch on this problem briefly in the Foreword of this book.)

If we consider the daughters and granddaughters of the women mentioned so far, who are called millennials in their 20s and 30s, we already encounter another kind of confusion. On both sides of the Atlantic, women of this age group today form a major clientele for psychological help, looking for a way out of confusions in instinctive and sexual life. The enormous step that women took to achieve freedom from biological destiny with the help of birth-control devices over half a century ago does not seem to hold the hope and advantage that it once did. A woman's struggle today is not simply to keep herself free from pregnancies and to develop her other potentials. Her concern is to somehow maintain a balance among her various needs and potentials. The control of the birth of her children is not so vital a problem as the control of theirs and her own life. She needs to know how to reap satisfaction from being a mother or a professional woman. The confusion with regard to one's choices (perhaps because of the many outer choices) about whether or not to have pregnancies, to adopt or to be pregnant in vitro including other alternatives such as surrogating, makes this important decision a problem. Then sometimes one changes one's mind and this often leads to an increasing number of voluntary abortions and further confusion and suffering as a result. Let me give an example.

I once had a client, a woman of thirty who came to therapy because of her problem with her boyfriend. Two years into the therapy she confessed that she had five abortions because each time the pregnancy was with the wrong person, sometimes a result of a one-night-stand. She spoke in a matter-of-fact tone but her emotional suffering for these unborn children began to show up in her dream images over a period of a whole year. She was shocked by her own reaction to these images. It took her another year to mourn her actions before she could be free of this painful chapter and a transformative change took place in herself. She realized that a choice whether to terminate a pregnancy or not is not so simple. She needed to know her emotional life better before indulging in casual sex without protection. For a modern and liberated woman the contradictory behavior of not using protection while having sex with unsuitable partners was indeed an enigma that she needed to understand about herself.

Similar confusions are observed in the area of marriage. If a young woman decides to "live together" with a young man she loves because she does not believe in marriage, after a few years she is not so sure that she is so satisfied by the arrangement. Should she have a child, or shouldn't she? Should she have the child with him without being married or with someone else or even by artificial insemination? If she wants a child, then perhaps it would be best to be married after all. It would be easier for the child and the parents and grandparents, etc. A woman in her late 20s or early 30s today has more choices as far as her choice of profession but hardly any choice not to have a choice — although having a job for an educated middle-class woman is no longer a matter of choice but a necessity. In most parts of Western Europe and America, sheer economic necessity pushes a woman to the job market to supplement the family income. This necessity is different from her poor counterpart in the sense that the former needs extra income to keep up the increasingly higher standard of living plus to enhance her self image of financial independence. She does not always have to choose between marriage and a profession as her mother and grandmother did. Marriage can be complementary to her profession, or it along with motherhood can be postponed until a later date, thanks to the advanced reproductive technology today.

Archetypes Live Through Changing Roles

From the viewpoint of her schooling of several years and its utilization, today's women are definitely better off compared with their mothers. Most women who seek work outside the home have opportunities to use some of the skills they learned at college and university. The young woman of today spends several hours of her day in the atmosphere of work, ideas and organization – the dealings of men. Her intellectual and organizing animus, which was nurtured at school, finds some useful expression this way. Hopefully, she can continue to use her disciplined thinking in a job where the application of such abilities is necessary. Her natural need to relate to people may be fulfilled in professions in medicine, teaching, social work, therapy and counseling. The establishment of departments of Human Services in most companies and corporations seems to recognize such innate feminine or human needs, which benefits the companies as well. The fact that larger numbers of women are engaged in the so-called helping professions (nursing, medicine, psychotherapy, social work, teaching, etc.) today, may indicate that working with people still offers more satisfaction than other careers for women. This trend may very well be the beginning of a tradition. However, these women also complain about being exhausted from multi-tasking. If they have children they end up being "superwoman," a status that cannot be sustained for long.

In the case of women who are being very successful in so-called masculine professions, it is possible that the identification with the animus I mentioned earlier continues beyond the school years, and a satisfaction is achieved. Such women enjoy rising to high positions, wielding power over other people, and making important decisions and contributions. The excitement of competition toward professional ambitions seems to sustain them, at least for several years. If I am correct in my speculation regarding the need for the archetype to live through human experience in both identification and projection (so that introjections can take place), then sooner or later such a woman feels pressure from within, perhaps reflected in many outer problems and crises, to project or to identify with another aspect of the animus. A neurotic or even a psychotic problem may be generated at this stage of life if she remains stuck too long in one phase, beyond the necessity of her psychological adaptation. Outer problems in jobs or relationships may also appear to make a shift essential as well, as documented in books such as *Cost of Loving* and *Women on Top*, mentioned earlier in this book.[33]

All cultures, through expected stages of life and through institutions and customs offer the possibilities of realizing the changing needs of our archetypal life. Despite exceptions, such prescriptions seem not only viable but necessary for both intellectual and emotional fulfillment. However, the forms and shapes the institutions take can change through time, as we are witnessing today. For example, it is quite possible for a Western woman today, albeit with some difficulty still, to combine marriage and a profession. Thus both her feminine and masculine archetypes may find simultaneous expressions in life.

As she finishes her schooling, one of the first choices a young woman in America makes is to look for a job and for a relationship, if not a husband right away. However, the high divorce rate indicates that marriages and remarriages are quite common despite the occasional fashionable practice of avoiding marriage for a few years. I already discussed many psychosocial aspects of modern marriage as an institution. Here, before giving an example of an individual case, I want to pay attention to "falling in love" as an alleged primary condition that precedes nearly all marriages in the Western world today. Millennial women and men do not seem to agree that love is the reason they marry. They not only use electronic means of search and communication to find a partner but also say that having an earning partner in life makes it easier economically and emotionally to navigate their post-cyber revolutionary lifestyle, which is complicated, ambitious, and expensive. Interestingly enough, back in 1973-74 when I conducted a survey among 300 married couples in Colorado, U.S.A., they said that the most important reason for their marriages was love. Responses from both men and women among 300 participants were unanimous.

Love and Marriage

Psychologists, like other scholars, rarely talk about "love" because it is impossible to reduce this unique experience into tangible units of ideas as an explanation. One cannot explain or understand love. Love in its various forms and intensities is a *mysterium tremendum* that grips us and lifts us above and beyond our usual existence. For a few moments or more, we are touched by the transcendence of the divine experience. A social institution such as marriage is only a feeble frame to contain romantic love since marriage as a practicing institution became customary long before what we call "romantic love" was recognized and recorded in human history. Yet, most married people still say that they marry because they are in love!

Love between a man and a woman seems to be the most intense and problematic of all the forms of love perhaps because this experience incorporates several archetypal needs at the same time. This kind of love first blossoms in adolescence, when both body and psyche are at a critical transition, releasing sex hormones as well as imaginations and fantasies. Most of our literature and art try to capture this mysterious experience in space and time. The tremendous poignancy of our pleasures and pains, success and disappointments in love seems to be the major moving force in our lives. Love that descends on us as an overwhelming emotion is the result of an archetype (the god of love Eros' arrow piercing the heart is an apt image), and the danger is unpredictable. For a short while two human beings are totally at the mercy of the archetypes or gods. Soon, sometimes too soon for our taste, separation must follow, as if to balance this dangerously disorienting, albeit pleasurable experience. In no other human experience is the alternation of union and separation so closely felt to each other as in the intense experience of love, especially in love between two young people. If we do not know why love grips us, at least we can remember that the pair of opposites (namely, union-separation) is close together as an archetypal basis for love.

A brief visual image of what I am trying to convey impressed me at the railway station one day when a young couple in love were separating from each other. While they were in a close embrace kissing to say good-bye, the train was announced to be a few minutes late. As soon as the announcement was heard, their embraced loosened a bit, and the young man, over the head of his lover, kept looking at the overhead clock. The young woman seemed a bit uneasy, as if the delay disrupted the predicted rhythm of their behavior suddenly. This delay in the anticipated separation cut the thread of their feelings unexpectedly. As the train appeared, everything seemed all right again. Their embrace was as intense and emotional now that the separation was a certainty.

Success of the greatest of our love stories and art forms seems to depend on expressing this dual sentiment and emotion well. I elaborate on this aspect of love before I talk about marriage because the institution of marriage as a social and cultural framework of the expected continuation of love offers the best example of the interplay of this dualism. Indeed its instability and failure may be directly connected to the balance and imbalance of the two poles of union and separation of the same archetype. Also, in this play of union-separation, the animus and anima, along with the outer woman and man, are significant actors on both the personal and transpersonal levels.

I have already touched on the idea that the increasing frequency of divorce in today's marriages may reflect the need for separation between the partners and their own contrasexual aspects, not just the outer separation between the partners. When a woman falls in love and, after a few months or years, decides to marry her lover, psychologically she is already acting contrary to the nature of love unless she and her lover are aware and prepared for drastic changes in their relationship. Marriage as a social and legal institution can only offer a framework to allow the romantic love to end, yet to continue in continuously moving forms, as all the jokes regarding honeymoon indicate.

Apart from the fact that falling in love is a mystery activated by the most powerful archetypes, the projection of particular aspects of the animus on the outer man is vital in this experience. In her book *The Way of All Women*, Esther Harding observes what may happen to a woman in love thus:

> "... the power and attraction of the animus are such that she is compelled, even against her will, to return to it again and again, just as a woman who, having fallen in love with a man who has represented animus to her and having resolved never to repeat the experience, is nonetheless irresistibly drawn into another affair which is a duplication of the first. Her burnt fingers do not save her any more than singed wings save the moth from the flame."[32]

This obsessive quality in the projection of the animus by a woman (or the anima by a man) may be the indicator that she must connect with her own inner self, her unconscious, and her own masculinity. I suspect the same woman may fall in love again and again to reconnect to either the same aspect or some very unknown aspects of herself. This urge is so urgent because it serves to open the way to individuation, another inevitable event that comes to us just like love. We have no choice but to surrender to it. In some cases such urges care little for social and moral dictates, and the animus may continue to lure a woman into projection after projection as the ghostly lover who is never realized in reality. Marriage may help to bring the illusion down to reality – an essential process toward humanization of the ghostly lover or the Prince Charming.

The well-known psychoanalyst and scholar Erik Erikson makes a significant observation that the emphasis on female fidelity in most cultures has to do with a woman's biological, psychological, and ethical commitment to take care of the infant.[33] I wonder if this question of sexual fidelity in a marriage, even before the appearance of a child or in a childless union, does not indicate a commitment to allow the animus to be experienced through the relationship within one committed framework. It may also be connected to the funneling of energy that includes most of one's sexual libido. Some couples become parents very quickly (like the woman quoted in the last chapter) to bind their illusory projections in the biological role of parent, letting the lover/animus subside for a while, only to come back in full force later in the middle of life. And then, of course, the animus can be experienced in a negative, compulsive, and destructive way.

One must also remember that in every marriage, the other side of union, i.e., separation, has to be realized sometimes by the projection of the negative aspect of the animus, as if the animus must live out its full course by going through both positive and negative poles. In a modern marriage, where it is mostly the married couple who lives alone, the partners must carry also the negative projections of the contrasexual archetypes. In cultures where a married couple shares the space with many other relatives, the pressure to carry the negative projections may not oppress the partners. Neither the husband's nor the wife's energy seems to be engaged primarily in each other. The family with many members reflects various unconscious elements of a woman, and her psychic health is maintained by both positive and negative projections on her family members.

In his book *Marriage Dead or Alive*, Adolf Guggenbühl-Craig claims and demonstrates through different images how marriage offers a framework for individuation and the salvation of the souls of the partners, but not necessarily for happiness or any other kind of fulfillment, such as a necessity for procreation, the legitimization of children's paternity, economic dependency, or sexual satisfaction. Still, people not only get married but seem to have viable marriages, which may appear neurotic, problematic, unhappy, and even "perverse."[34] Basing his observations on many years of analytical practice, Guggenbühl-Craig observes that the psychological meaning of a modern marriage has to do with the partners' individuation, the unconscious force that brings and keeps them together.

I would like to add to the above view that marriage, as one of the oldest institutions of human societies has become a psychological entity, an archetypal form as it were, and it is a vital framework for the contrasexual aspects of the partners to be lived through, suffered, enjoyed, and in the process humanized. This is a framework that may last from 50 to 70 years of one's life (even with more than one partner), where the projection of the animus and anima takes place again and again, leading toward further assimilation and the eventual individuation of the partners. No other relationship seems to offer such an arena for these processes to be realized and lived out.

However, because of the struggle that a modern marriage must go through to fulfill this goal, many young people opt not to marry. It is quite common today for a couple to live together, often for a period of several years, and even have a family, since legalization of children's paternity is not a problem any more, at least in many Western countries. The pressure of negative projection onto the partners seems stronger within the framework of marriage, and it is easier not to involve oneself in the legal and other social intricacies if one must escape such a pressure. What Guggenbühl-Craig suggests seems to require a persevering attitude, which presupposes a more mature psychological consciousness regarding the archetypal background of the marriage by the partners themselves. On the other hand, we also witness an increasing relaxation in divorce laws and a greater social acceptance of both single and divorced individuals. It is quite possible that we are witnessing a transition — a change in the archetype of marriage itself. Only time will tell.

At this point, let me follow the course of a particular marriage briefly to see how the archetypes dictate the ongoing play.

Elizabeth's Marriage

A woman of 34, whom I shall call Elizabeth, had a father who was a famous scientist. He was brilliant, successful, interesting, and affectionate. Elizabeth's mother was also successful in her own right. She was a professional musician and an attractive woman. Their only daughter, Elizabeth had shown more inclination toward her father's talent and seemed to be much closer to her father. At age 29, Elizabeth married a young man, also a bright scientist, who worked as her father's research assistant for a while. Elizabeth had already established herself as a bright and creative scientist, and her research was already known in the particular branch of science she worked. With her parent's approval their marriage began smoothly. They were offered good positions at the same university where her father was a professor, although in two different departments. Everybody envied them their luck.

Obviously, Elizabeth projected a strong and positive animus on her young, bright husband, as she had projected the same on her father. But the husband, who did not mind such adoration, also knew instinctively somehow that marrying the daughter of a famous and admirable man might create some problems. But he, too, fell in love and enjoyed the position of being the enviable husband of such an intelligent, attractive woman. When their marriage was slightly over two years old, some difficulties began to arise. It seemed as if Elizabeth had to realize something more than just the admirable husband in the young man. She began to find faults with him, and gradually a stronger, negative side began to emerge in her, as if she needed to see herself and her husband both as ordinary people who could be mean and nasty. A primitive shadow of her admirable father and perhaps an equally unspiritual and banal animus of the very polished mother began to rear their heads, and the woman knew nothing of what was happening, except to blame her husband for many things. Her provocation often succeeded in getting him into the negative role, and they ended up having severe fights. There were, of course, outer events to account for all this, but being fairly intelligent people, the couple also realized that they had little control over what was happening. Elizabeth's separation from her secure parental home and losing her father's stimulating, affectionate company had something to do with it also. The husband found the situation totally unpredictable, despite all his apprehensions at marrying such a woman. He came close to collapse. His emotional survival seemed to depend on his occasional ability to withdraw from the scene, only to be goaded and attacked with some new excuses. He, too, realized that they were under bigger forces than themselves.

They both led busy professional lives, and it was absolutely imperative for them to come to terms with the destructive situation. Elizabeth was very surprised by her own nature, something she never suspected she could be. This state of affairs continued for over nine months, and they began to talk about seeking some professional help. They talked about it when both of them were relatively calm but later they became furious and hateful toward each other. One surprising thing still kept them together, and that was the intense attraction they still felt for one another. In between their nasty fights, they would come vigorously close, sexually and emotionally. The sexual contact became more intense as the struggle intensified. The negative pole of the archetype also opened the instinctive pole of the living experience for these two people who lived more in their brilliant minds than in their bodies. If they did not go into their vigorous struggles and fights, perhaps the dormant sexuality would not have opened up.

This kind of destructive situation could not continue for long. Their professional lives demanded some sanity and composure. The husband began to crack up first. He was very happy when he got an invitation to attend a conference in London and leave the country for a few weeks. Both of them felt a sense of relief at this separation. Interestingly enough, they never thought of a legal separation amid all this turmoil. Their involvement with each other was much too strong; they were bound together by a destructive marriage. In London the husband ran into an old friend, a divorcee whom he had known nearly 10 years earlier. A few drinks and dinner followed by mutual confessions brought them close, and Elizabeth's husband felt a great release of pressure as he continued to be with the other woman, who was not as attractive, as bright, or as difficult as Elizabeth. Obviously, both of them needed someone's shoulder to cry on.

Elizabeth, in the meantime, spent the time alone, trying to sort out things a bit in her own mind and gained a little more perspective. She went to see a girlfriend who was a therapist and had a heart-to-heart talk. She made a resolution to persuade her husband to go for professional help also and she wanted to ask his forgiveness and admit all her stupidity and faults. She realized how unreasonable and obnoxious she had been. She prepared herself to greet her husband as in the old days and even telephoned her parents after many months and told her mother that she would like to get pregnant. She also wrote a draft letter to her department for a year's leave of absence during which time she planned to go into therapy. Elizabeth waited with trepidation to welcome her husband back after three weeks.

Her husband, after his arrival and sensing some changes in the atmosphere, did not give his wife a chance to open her mouth before declaring his newfound love. For some sadistic reason or other, or just to avenge himself, he went into great detail about the new woman and their wonderful time together. He also confessed that he never really loved Elizabeth; perhaps he was dazzled by the glamour of his in-laws and by her brilliant mind. But he needed something else.

The blow came when she expected it least. Somehow the shock of it woke her up from the other, unreal world they had been living in. Elizabeth broke down physically. She had to be hospitalized with what was diagnosed as a nervous breakdown. Then the real suffering began. Gradually, she began to realize that the life she knew was not real. As an attractive, successful daughter of a famous father and an attractive professional mother, she had never really known what failure was. Even her fights with her husband for over a year were not as bad as his rejection. Her looks, education, professional success, and intelligence — none of it helped to save her marriage. She had lost, lost miserably to a less educated and ordinary woman. Her shame, anger, and bitterness kept her incapable of functioning in everyday life, and she had no choice but to stay in bed in a dark room of the hospital, helped and cared for by professional nurses.

Several months later slowly and gradually, Elizabeth began to regain herself. The pain and anger that she had felt after her husband's departure now became only a void. She felt rather light, as one feels after a long night's sleep. The stabbing pain that pierced her every time she thought about her marriage failed to hurt now, to her great relief. Perhaps the wound had healed. She gained a sense of self-worth during those months of suffering and she was still not sure what this really meant. Somehow, all her shame and loss and pain seemed to have melted into something like "it really does not matter anymore." This was the time when I met her, and she literally shrugged at the topic. She told me her story over a number of days, and I could see that much of the anger and hate were gone from her narration.

She came to see me to discuss the possibility of finding an analyst because she felt she needed to know herself more. During her illness, she discovered something she still did not understand clearly. She needed a guide to take her somewhere that promised more peace and less struggle. I was struck by her ways. She seemed to have aged immensely and appeared a bit lost. She also shared two dreams with me that she had dreamed while in the hospital and that had stayed with her. The first dream:

> I am in a car with my father in the driver's seat. As we drive quite fast on the highway, I notice it's actually my husband who is driving the car. Suddenly he pulls off the highway because there's an accident that took place in front of us. As he gets out of our car a huge truck-like vehicle rushes in and hits him. I see his bloody body lying on the road. To my horror both his hands are crushed.

The second dream was dreamed after she was released from the hospital, and this dream left her with a strong emotion and somehow made her think of analysis:

> I am with several women, among whom are my two grand-mothers (who are dead), my husband's girlfriend (whom I do not know), and two very ugly, lower-class women. We take a hike together toward a valley. I seem to go with the two ugly women ahead of the others. The two women walk ahead of me and do not say a word. I feel a bit nervous yet excited and full of curiosity. I wake up with a strange sense of excitement."

She told me that during her illness, she often had dreams where the instruments in her laboratory seemed to be broken or turned into animals or food vessels. Interestingly enough, these dreams were the first things that took her mind away from her bitterness against her husband. She was grateful for the dream images for this reason, although she did not understand what the dreams meant.

It was interesting to me that she chose to tell me the two dreams, one indicating the dismemberment of her driving animus by a bigger autonomous force, and the other showing the emergence of many feminine shadows, some of whom seemed helpful and guiding. Only after the sacrifice of the active animus could her unknown yet helpful feminine aspects emerge. Her emotional reaction to the second dream was also significant. The appearance of her two grandmothers and her husband's lover added a special creative potential to the second dream. I felt her door to individuation had already opened through her colossal marital crisis and her quiet suffering in the hospital. In the case of Elizabeth, who developed her intellectual animus extremely well, the guiding and potentially creative shadow had remained primitive, undeveloped and unattractive up to that point. The striking appearance even of her husband's girlfriend in the dream shows that she may even be ready to connect to her much-hated rival shadow.

Betrayal in Marriage

In the story of Elizabeth's marriage crisis, the appearance of a second woman triggered the final break and the wife's breakdown, which in retrospect seemed to offer her the first step toward intro- version. What indeed is the psychological significance of this age-old phenomenon of the other woman or the love triangle?

Literature and history abound in examples where jealous husbands or irate wives cause havoc and destruction on all sides, along with a lot of suffering. Indeed, the love triangle is an archetypal pattern that seems to come into being whenever a pair of lovers believes in nothing but bliss and happiness. In a penetrating and moving article titled "Betrayal," James Hillman discusses how breaking the naive trust by a partner or lover may lead to the development of the contrasexual (the anima in his article) archetype through bitter suffering.[35] Hillman suggests (and I agree) that betrayal by one of the partners may be the only way a woman (or a man) may become aware of her (his) projected and neglected animus (anima). Elizabeth projected her animus onto her father and then onto her husband. When the negative pole of the archetype began to make trouble, she projected that onto him too. Only through an act of betrayal on her husband's part could she be thrown back on herself and realize that she owned some of the virtues and vices she was projecting onto others. Fortunately for her, the physical breakdown prevented her from acting out further; otherwise she could easily have been led by her very active animus to go for revenge, a common reaction after a marriage or love betrayal.

Jealousy that is not endured but is acted out in revenge creates further problems, even leading to evil actions. Life and literature are full of Othellos and Lady Murasakis, who create devastation because of the unconsciousness of their own psyches and their inability to suffer with their own deficiencies. Like love — and often following love — jealousy also descends on us, and we have no choice but to live and suffer through it. Only then we learn to acknowledge and accept our darkness, which gives us a tolerance to others' failings, along with a deeper understanding of ourselves. Unfortunately the literature seldom captures stories of the characters who suffer and endure consciously invariably arriving to a peaceful transcendence when the negative aspect of the archetype is integrated.

In marriage or in a love relationship, the other man or woman can therefore be a godsend for those partners who need such a blow to become conscious of themselves. The other woman, as in Elizabeth's dream, can also offer the first possibility of ego's acknowledgement of the worst shadow. To her great surprise, the betrayed woman may begin to believe that she needed the other woman as much as her husband. This is another opportunity for a woman to see her most neglected side, since a strong hate and jealousy have already opened the door to emotional contact with her shadow side. Therefore, a betrayal that precipitates pain and suffering can help a woman connect with both her animus and shadow. The entrance of a new woman into the dyad of a couple is also an outer reflection of the inner struggle of the contrasexual sides of the partners. The following diagram may show these various struggles a bit clearer:

WIFE ——————————————————————————— **HUSBAND**
Outer struggle / Projection

ANIMUS ·· **ANIMA**
Connection in the Unconscious

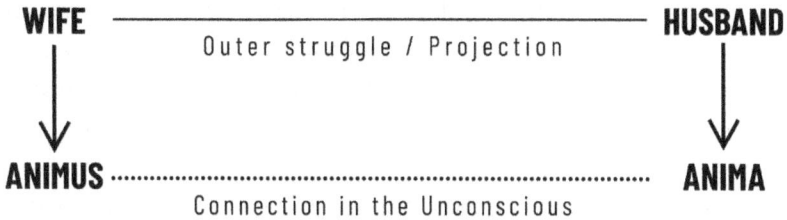

Only after the partners suffer through the separation may the withdrawal of the projections be completed and, hopefully internalization with one's own contrasexual element (or some elements) can take place. As long as life goes on, this process is followed by newer identifications and projections to be withdrawn in their due course. The second woman, or man, in a marriage, therefore, is only another carrier of projection of a new element that the partner fails to carry. As far as the 'other woman' is concerned her suffering may teach her to look at her motives of being involved with an unavailable man. It's possible that she is a 'Hetaira' (see page 109) and likes to remain in an undefined relationship with a man or she suffers from a fear of commitment. At any rate she also has an opportunity to transform if she allows herself to enter the triangle seriously and suffers from humiliation and pain of guilt.

Let me reiterate that, whatever the structural analysis of the love triangle may be (whether we try to understand the dynamics with the help of animus- anima projection or any other), the emotional impact from such an experience is crucial for all three concerned. The fire that burns all three people ranges from disappointment, jealousy, anger, and revenge to guilt, hurt, and shame. When honestly acknowledged, faced, and endured, negative emotions are less destructive and may even be constructive. In the case of Elizabeth, these emotions helped her find a connection to her undeveloped femininity. The threat of losing the possibility of union with her husband, her opposite, had to come from a new union, this time a union within herself, with other neglected and perhaps even despised sides of herself, personified by the ugly women in the second dream and the 'other woman' her husband chose.

Reactions to a betrayal in love and marriage vary from woman to woman. For those to whom the outer symbol of union has become an entity in itself, the animus begins to create irritation because the real purpose of the marriage remains unknown to the partners. This is the way the projected animus can be withdrawn so that the painful emotions associated with the experience can be interjected. And the same animus can now help her and guide her to her inner work. The transcendent function can only come about through the avalanche of pain and suffering.

Motherhood: Wanda

So far, I have discussed a marriage that was only two years old when difficulties began to arise and a betrayal by the husband opened the door to the wife's suffering and individuation. What happens to a woman who is married for many years, has children, and remains a wife/mother without much apparent difficulty? We also saw Emily's case briefly in the last chapter where, as a 48-year-old married woman after 20 years of childbearing and rearing, she suddenly woke up to the realization that she has been deceived by life. A sense of being lost permeated her life. I contacted Emily again while writing this book's first draft over a decade later and found out that the choices she made were not something I expected from her confessions then. By 1982, Emily became a serious alcoholic. She was still married to the same man but was no more frustrated, nor was she even aware of the waste of her talents. Her husband lived his own life and left Emily alone to her addiction.

The problem Emily saw in 1971 points to a general pattern that many mothers share. In a well-researched book, *Women of a Certain Age: The Midlife Search for Self* (1979), Lillian B. Rubin documents how the mothers react to the empty-nest crisis when the children are grown and leave home. Among 160 women between the ages of 35 and 54 who were interviewed in this book, many took this crisis as a challenge and found a new identity beyond motherhood. However, the first shock of the crisis and the painful process of newfound identity are extremely difficult for some women, who, like Emily, never succeed in coping.

Like Emily, some intelligent women with good intellectual promise in youth have conscious plans to build careers, yet fall into marriage and motherhood as if something stronger inside had moved them in this direction. Yet they fail to enjoy mothering perhaps because mothering is not what they are really suited for. Secondly, once in the role, some of them play the role perfectly as they may have played the role of good student earlier. They are indoctrinated by collective ideals of good wife/mother roles early and they work hard at being *what they should be rather than what they are meant to be.* Individuality in the real sense is sacrificed to an ideal that may come from the mother, the family, or just the time and fashion. A false persona identified with a collective image that is not founded in her instinct offers her satisfaction only for a limited time. That is why women like Emily feel lost and betrayed by life after a while.

If the intellectual animus with highly creative potential cannot be projected out onto the husband or children, the result can be quite destructive. Such an archetype can turn into a demonic force creating various problems often manifested in psychosomatic ailments or other variants. In practice I encounter women in their 40s with serious complaints of asthma, rheumatism, migraine and other symptoms, if not addiction or depression. Many of them have pasts and personalities similar to that of Emily's. Is it possible, then, that if the intellectually active animus is identified with in early years, it cannot be projected out and must be lived out and incorporated in life? Women who spend years of hard work bringing up children can be quite lazy when it comes to using their minds and dormant talents unless pushed and encouraged by someone or something. Sometimes, husbands and children become instrumental in helping the woman make the first move, or a crisis such as husband's betrayal or divorce may do it for others.

Women who find it impossible to respond to the demands of the changed circumstances of the empty nest after years of marriage and mothering represent the somewhat fossilized aspect of the feminine archetype in its rather archaic form. Such a woman who is determined to keep a status quo at any cost is actually ruled by a selfish and manipulative animus perhaps in cahoots with an equally primitive shadow since she lacks the ego strength nurtured by the positive and transformative feminine archetype. She manages to find friends or ideas that carry the projections of the manipulative and negative aspects of the archetypes to help her in her determination not to rock the boat. If the husband breaks this destructive alliance by some action on his part, she then is left without not only security but also an identity, albeit a false one. She can go on the rest of her life blaming her husband or others for her misfortune unless she is able to suffer honestly enough to initiate a change of attitude.

Women who are natural wives and mothers and play both roles well have the risk of falling into what I like to call the "identification of the archaic feminine archetype" when mothering ends. Following is such an example. By living her masculine side totally through her husband and sons, Wanda also betrayed her own femininity. She remained stuck to the very archaic maternal identity, causing destruction around her.

Wanda is 48 and has three children between the ages of 20 and 25. She married a young law school graduate when she was 20 before finishing college herself. Her husband is now a successful divorce lawyer. She has been very busy and active in bringing up her three children and helping her husband build a career by shouldering all the household chores herself. She is intelligent, efficient, and attractive. Everyone, including Wanda herself, thought she was one of the luckiest women until five years ago, when problems began to develop like storm clouds in her clear, sunny life. Their daughter, the youngest child who was then 15, along with a group of friends, was found to be involved in taking drugs and committing petty crimes. Six months of agony, shame, and battle between the parents and the daughter yielded nothing; the girl ran away several times until at 18 she moved out and became involved with a drug-pusher. Wanda was totally shattered by this turn of events for over three years. Then one day as she was sorting laundry, a letter fell out of her husband's pants pocket, exposing of an affair he had been having with a divorcée. In fact, Wanda knew about this woman, who was her husband's client in a divorce case. After the initial shock,

Wanda pretended as if nothing had happened. A few weeks later when she confronted him, he tried to evade the topic by saying that it was nothing but a fling, a diversion from all the troubles with their daughter. Although the letter could not have been written too long ago, Wanda did not dare find out if the diversion was continuing.

She told no one except her boys, the two older children who were both at university. She kept up the social façade as before, mostly spending more time with the younger boy who was in the area studying at the same law school his father attended. She stopped sharing the bedroom with her husband but never raised the subject of the other woman again. After six months, her husband told her that he wanted a legal separation because Wanda's silence was getting on his nerves. Wanda was very much surprised that her tolerance of his betrayal was not even appreciated. She flatly refused to have any open break. It would ruin the boys, she argued. The boys, as a matter of act, did object to a divorce because they knew that the mother would be absolutely lonely and they did not want the responsibility to having to take care of her.

The husband, however, went ahead with the divorce proceedings, and Wanda had no choice but to contest. She got the best divorce lawyer in the state, a family friend and a man who felt great sympathy for the wife who did nothing to deserve such cruelty after 28 years of marriage. He fought hard, and Wanda managed to have all their tangible property and a sizable alimony for life, which she had to sacrifice after a year by marrying her lawyer, who had a substantially higher income than that of the ex-husband.

A year after her second marriage, Wanda's second husband came to see me for a referral to a therapist for himself. He was facing considerable difficulties with his wife and stepsons, who kept in close contact with them. When Wanda heard this, she wanted to see me as well, and it was mostly from her that I heard her story. She denied any marital problems except that her second husband was unreasonably jealous of her sons who, incidentally, were still unmarried at 34 and 32. Her husband also wanted her to take a job outside the home, as if she did not have enough to do. She did not understand why her husband was unhappy, because she was very content and busy looking after her husband and two sons, of whom she was very proud. She paused with a smile of surprise on her lips. I saw how futile it would be to remind her of her wayward daughter and her two unhappy husbands. She was too unconscious to have any insights into herself. She was determined not to rock the boat of her selfish existence despite all the turmoil around her. The last I heard was that Wanda's second husband moved out of the house and the younger son moved in.

Little has been said so far about the normal mothering process where a woman is satisfied being a mother and does not grudge the sacrifices she makes for several years of her life. On the other hand, she does not cling to her children for her own security thus keeping them bound to her unconsciously by projecting her unfulfilled ambitions onto them. A mother like this develops other interests besides her children in her later years and can retire from motherhood gracefully to develop some impersonal or spiritual interests, and or may become a doting grandmother.

The pleasure and suffering that a mother must undergo are not only connected to her bio-physical role of a mother who must sacrifice years of her life and then withdraw from the life of adult children, but also to our time, which seems to values motherhood less and less. If we compare this situation in the West with a less developed country (economically) such as India, the odds against a mother in the West are even more visible. In India, a woman's self-worth is intricately connected to her becoming a mother (especially of a son), and her projection on her son(s) continues throughout her life until she is a grandmother and is ready to project on the child-god and a guru, a religious guide. The satisfaction she receives from being a mother is added to by the tremendous value her culture and tradition place on this role, even today. [36]

For a Western mother, the support and respect from her society and culture are only marginal. Just as her physical difficulties during childbirth are minimized by advanced medical means, the psychological and instinctive satisfactions of motherhood also become less important.

Indeed, the length of time required to build a career among other factors like the awareness of increasing population pressure in the world may make a modern educated woman less inclined to choose motherhood.

Does this mean, perhaps, that for a woman of modern Western society, her animus cannot be realized only through her family? She must separate from such projections even before she becomes a grandmother, if indeed she ever does. The pressure for a mother to live out her masculine potential outside the orbit of her children and husband is stronger than ever before. Her own choice not to have many children, to free herself from engrossing mothering for many years, also demands that she does something with her life. She has many more years of active adult life left after her retirement from a job.

Other Alternatives

The challenge then is to use the remaining years of her life doing something for herself. A mother who is close to 60 and has three well-educated and well-placed children told me how she wished she had never had children. Her two daughters and one son — all quite successful — live away from her and rarely call or visit. She does not even know how many grandchildren she has. She wishes she knew where and how she went wrong in her mothering. For her son and daughter-in-law, she is nothing but a nuisance. The daughters are not interested in marriage or motherhood. Is this situation her problem, or is it the times? She asks.

On the other hand, there are not only more opportunities today for a mother to use her energy and time in other occupations and interests, but even traditional mothering can transform into something more spiritual and meaningful by combining activities or professions incorporating mothering in different ways. The Swiss psychoanalyst Toni Wolff's article "Structural Forms of the Feminine Psychology" poses four psychic forms for a modern woman of Wolff's time, i.e. the mid-20th century.[37]

According to Wolff, a woman in the first part of her life, lives one of the four following psychological roles. This is only a schematic sketch, therefore, not to be taken as fully realistic.

Wife / Mother

Medial woman ──────────── **Amazon**

Hetaira or Companion

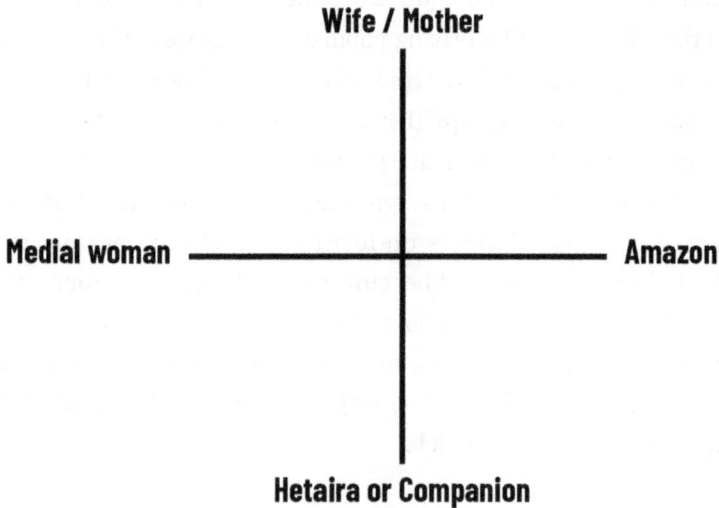

The psychological characteristics of each role can be briefly describes as follows:

Wife/Mother: She lives in concrete reality arranging, organizing, and administering the space and food for her family and others. She can order and structure her environment to the benefit of her family's survival. She is attuned to the earth and lunar cycle, therefore more aware of a natural timing, tact, and rhythm. She is sensitive to others' needs and responds to situations in concrete and practical terms rather than abstract ways. In her negative aspect, she is reluctant to change and to be conscious, and her capacity to nurture can turn into a means to control. A woman who acts in this role predominantly, usually carries the projection of the collective aspect of the Mother Archetype.

Hetaira, a Greek word that means a female companion: She is a companion and friend to both men and women in a pleasurable and inspiring way without the dependence of a negative mother. Pleasing rather than nurturance is more important to her. Relationships seem illusive, and she is attractive to others because of that. She seems to be the opposite of the wife/mother. A Hetaira may very likely live out the androgynous quality of the collective animus, which is no longer unconscious. She has made a living connection to her contrasexual side.

Amazon: Like the Greek mythological figure, an Amazon is capable of being independent of all relationships with men, although she is strongly influenced by men's ideas and convictions. She is not reluctant to change and is quick in pioneering new activities. She is also able to respond to abstract situations with abstract ideas. She can be ruthless in following an ideal. In her extreme form, she is the determined career woman who is ready to sacrifice emotional relationships. An Amazon is unconscious of her total identification with the collective aspect of the animus archetype.

Medial Woman: Medial woman is the most intuitive of all and is capable of grand visions of collective life and is in touch with the feminine mystery more than others. She is the mediumistic healer or priestess, inspired artist. In her negative manifestation she can easily be a hysterical borderline personality. She can be creative in many areas and can inspire a group or a nation by her special capacity to be connected to the impersonal situations and ideas in a grand style. In her negative aspect, she becomes only a carrier for collective projections and may run the risk of ending up as an empty vessel for such projections.

If a woman lives the role of the Mother/Wife predominantly, in the next phase she may have to live out either the Medial or Amazon, and the fourth, in this case Hetaira, may remain in her unconscious, only to express itself in a more primitive way. One or the other of the Medial or Amazon roles may be her close second, conscious psychological tendency. If she is predominantly a Mother/Wife and her second form is Amazon, both the Hetaira and Medial forms would remain unconscious until later in her life.

Wolff observed the above tendencies from her years of analytical practice with neurotic women in Switzerland during the first half of the 20th century. In view of the changed time in Western Europe and America today, I would like to propose a modified scheme that may be applied to the modern situation more closely.

A diagram like the following may express the changing times better, since many of the forms and roles are now overlapping and going through some transition, as has been discussed in this book. For example, a modern woman can live her Hetaira qualities as a wife who is also a professional and a companion to her husband and other men. Or a mother with medial qualities can become a therapist or a professional medium, which are perfectly acceptable professions for an aging woman today. The modified diagram may look like this.

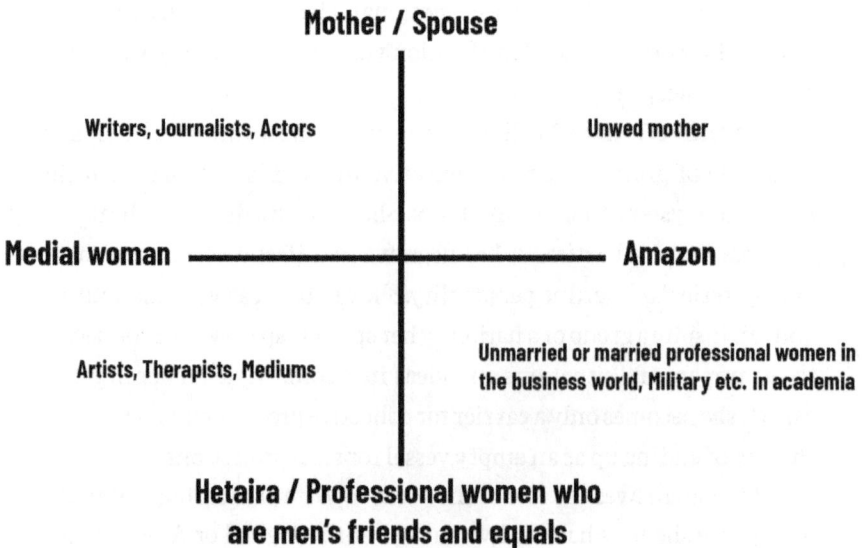

Mother / Spouse

Writers, Journalists, Actors   Unwed mother

Medial woman ———————————————— **Amazon**

Artists, Therapists, Mediums   Unmarried or married professional women in the business world, Military etc. in academia

**Hetaira / Professional women who
are men's friends and equals**

Even for an Amazon today, it is not necessary to deny or defy men totally. She can be married and still live out her Amazon qualities as well, depending on her husband's anima projections. The husbands of some of the most engaging professional women (political leaders, scientists, medical doctors, business executives, and military personnel) seem to manage to survive both physically and mentally! On the other hand, some of the modern young Amazons seem to have gone back to their warring nature like their mythological counterparts. Though a very recent tendency, some women seem to fit in this role well. A number of them go to the war front and court danger, leaving their young children behind to be cared for by their husbands or family members. Such a career choice, admittedly, is due to economic pressure. Joining the military right after high school has become a trend among young women from lower economic classes during last couple of decades.

Despite the changes of the past half a century, Wolff's scheme remains a useful tool in understanding some of the neurotic developments of a woman's psychology, because being in one role more than the others may result in an unhealthy imbalance in many cases. Such a structural scheme also helps us to see the archetypal background behind the forms influencing a woman's relationship to her outer world, men and women, and her inner world — her animus. Her dominant structural form may determine the quality of her relationships with her outer and inner men. Such a scheme can be used as a yardstick to determine the evolution within the life of a woman and in the psychological development of women in general.

Three decades after Wolff's formulation of the structure of the feminine psyche, in a publication titled *Goddesses in Every Woman: A New Psychology of Women* (1984), Jean Shinoda Bolen offers a different kind of structural understanding of a woman's psyche by using seven Greek goddesses representing different images within a woman. These images are categorized under aspects such as virgin goddess, vulnerable goddess and alchemical goddess all residing in each woman in different contexts and times of her life. By knowing one's own inner images, a woman can, the author suggests, discover her uniquely powerful inner pattern, which can help her overcome inhibiting traits toward realizing her full potential.

The great psychological contribution of Bolen's book lies in elaborating the myriad variations of the feminine archetype within the same woman in different contexts as well as in different women in the same context. A modern woman does not have to choose between being Hera and Aphrodite; she can be both and many others such as Athena, Artemis, Hestia, Demeter, and Persephone, depending on the particular combinations of the archetypes (represented by these goddesses) that are active at certain times within herself. However, mythological analogy may not always appeal to all women's emotional experience unless they are trained to do so or they come from cultures where myths are alive and part of everyday existence. In fact, one needs not always use the Greek goddesses to identify the various tendencies and potentials that are deeply rooted in the powerful archetypes. What Bolen and other feminist writers critically term control of social stereotypes in a woman's life may often be the only way to discover them within. Only by living the roles of one's social and cultural stereotypes can a woman realize the problems of living one archetype more or less than the other. Often difficulties in one role make the person "shift gears" toward realizing another potential or turn from one goddess to the next.

As an example of this interplay of several archetypal needs and the conscious ego on the one hand and the ego's submission to and rebellion against the social roles and cultural norms on the other, I cite the journal of a 40-year-old-woman. This woman had no psychological knowledge in the sense of having a theoretical understanding of herself when she wrote this journal in 1973 as a course assignment in an adult education class. Yet, she possessed a consciousness to assess and balance her life's outer demands and inner needs. She demonstrates a development of personality in keeping with her archetypal needs totally from her intuitive understanding of herself.

An Example of a Balanced Life

"I was born in the peak of Depression. My mother was 24 years of age when I was born. Financial straits, rather than a propensity for nursing, led her to seek that training. Upon graduation, she met my father who was two years older than she, extremely shy and reserved. He had only two years of college education but lacked money to complete his studies, a fact which he regretted for the rest of his life.

I was born the year following their marriage. At about three years of age I recall walks with my father, singing to him at his request often.

But, in those first years as well as later, my mother was the central figure in my life. She was, and is, a small, determined, humorous person. She laughed a great deal with her sister and her neighbors, my father hesitantly following with a shy smile. I am indebted to her for learning how to laugh and see the antic side of most situations. My father was unable to display affection openly. Both my two sisters and I felt constrained in his presence. These feelings were carried over into later years in encounters with other males. As a teenager my self-image was poor. I became a girl who was 'unpopular with boys' in a time when a girl's value was measured almost wholly in popularity terms.

At home, we had a good time with family rituals, holidays and vacation trips. My father showed his love in indirect ways. Often he stopped at the public library after work to choose, with great care, books for me. My principal recreation was reading. I devoured books and no prohibition was placed against what I might read. My school years went smoothly and without any problems as far as academic performances were concerned. I remained shy with boys and read a lot. I went to a Catholic girls' college. I must add here that one of the strongest forces that worked in my life was Catholicism. All of my life till then I accepted without question the restrictions imposed by the church. The greatest emphasis was on sexual morality. We were told that sexual indiscretions would doom one to eternal fires. Shortly before graduation, I was seriously intending to get married to a young man. One evening, however, I suddenly came to the realization that I could not spend the next forty or fifty years with him. And, with that, the promise was broken.

I decided to move to California and left for San Francisco with little idea as to what employment was available there. During a few interviews I was forced to guile and claimed secretarial skills I did not possess. I also realized that independence can be both intimidating and heartening. I learned to handle money, make decisions and speak for myself. After a year I became restless in a tedious job and became determined to travel in Europe. Within six months I was on a French liner and a six month odyssey which enriched me emotionally beyond measure.

When I returned home I spent two years in a succession of jobs, some unpromising, a few interesting. I never hesitated to leave a position when I became restless or possessed enough money to travel. It was upon taking a new job that I met my husband. He worked as an attorney in the same building as I. A few months after our first meeting he asked me and we were married.

Marriage was a profound shock. I remember the first two years as being one of subtle tensions and adjustments. My husband was twelve years older than I, divorced and a father of two children. He was educated, sophisticated and more generous and kind than I expected. I also found out soon that his strength could become domination. Soon he began to put pressures on me, mostly nonverbally, to be the total and perfect wife. I had to cook, entertain, handle my step-children well etc. This last item created a lot of tensions. The children had problems accepting me with their father and I was dismayed that instant maternal love did not blossom in my heart. Within two years of our marriage, without understanding exactly what was happening, I began to resist losing my 'personhood'. We did not have violent arguments, but I made it clear to him how I felt. Those were very difficult years. Slowly we developed a balance -- balance of power that we both needed and we struck many compromises, because we wanted to stay together.

Pregnancy was another shock. Within the first year of our marriage I was pregnant. When I learned it I felt a panic, akin to someone caught in a confining dangerous tunnel. These feelings gradually subsided and our son arrived without much complications. The mechanics of dealing with a baby's incessant requirements at first overwhelmed me, but I learned to deal with the reality as if I ceased to be a free agent. His care was the first consideration. It was a feeling I could not predict I possessed and mothering was one of the most gratifying experiences. Two years later I gave birth to our first daughter, and in another two years a second. Then despite my Catholic upbringing, we had to make some decisions about not having any more children. It took some doing on my part, and my husband was very helpful in convincing me in this regard. I learned to be practical and not to feel guilty because of an outmoded idea. All three of our children turned out to be rather open and affectionate people. I attribute their outgoing and loving nature to their father. My husband took a great deal of interest in the children when they were growing up.

When our youngest was three years old, I returned to the university to work towards a Master's degree in English literature. The reading and writing assignments were often threateningly enormous; but with the support of my family I could finish. I found out that despite the hard work, often through the late hours at night, my temper and mood improved with this engaging work. Even my husband and children remarked on this jokingly. I had hoped to teach following my degree, but somehow the market was overrun by people with similar or higher credentials than I had. It was disappointing, but I decided to devote myself to some creative writing on my own and also volunteered to instruct illiterates in the lower-class area of the city. Perhaps, my father's strong desire to continue his studies and his inability to do so has something to do with my own higher education and my desire to help others. Incidentally, my father was the only one who read my Master's thesis from cover to cover.

An interesting and sometimes disturbing element has entered my life in the last three or four years. The feminist movement caught some fire around me. The movement often appears to tell me that my values are wrong, my roles are farce, and my accomplishments as a wife and mother nothing. Yet, I know that without my life as a married woman and mother I may not have felt the inner pressure to go about my studies and work outside. The leisure and luxury of financial and emotional support that I received from my husband and family were essential for me. The domesticity that is so strongly criticized, paradoxically allowed me the freedom to pursue a variety of interests, not just studies.

I am not very clear about my niggling unease about this. Perhaps, it has to do with the suspicion in my own mind, that I allowed the major events of my adult life, i.e., marriage and the arrival of the children, to happen to me, rather than firmly charting a course and forging my own destiny. Yet, every turn of my life seemed to have done something significant for my growth and I must admit that my husband's companionship has been a vital force in this development. I have learned from him a greater warmth and generosity of spirit which has helped melt a certain coldness in my own nature. I like myself better now.

Addendum (written ten years later, in 1982)

The ten years elapsed have been eventful but kind. My father died after four years of terrible grip of a degenerative disease which created difficult problems of estrangements among the family members. I have become increasingly remote from my brother and sisters. My mother is sad by this. She, however, remains her usual vigorous and alert self and is finding solace in her religion which in its organized form leaves me more dissatisfied now than before. A solitary core which has always been part of my nature is possibly becoming more apparent with age.

I resumed my studies toward a Ph.D. in literature. In addition, I do a great deal of work recording for the blind which has introduced me to a wide variety of studies. My children are all working and studying and are scattered in various parts of the world right now. With the children's departure a matter of which I had been quite apprehensive, my marriage has grown stronger. Even if I worry over my children's whereabouts at times, I am usually content. My life is not the stuff of a great drama, but would I wish it otherwise? I await with interest the happenings of the next decade."

Brief Comments

This life story, which appears nearly ideal on paper, was chosen because it demonstrates how an ordinary life may flow naturally, allowing balanced interplay of the ego and the self via active cooperation with the animus. The trick was that the woman's ego always remained active, receptive, and aware. This woman may have been fortunate to inherit a stable combination of traits from her parents — an optimistic mother and a shy father who valued and encouraged education strongly. Her adolescence, guided by a stringent Catholic code, seemed to have helped her paradoxically to remain feminine in an instinctive way. The choice of marriage after college followed by a broken promise indicates an instinctive decision rather than a well-thought-out, calculated move. Such a sudden step can also be a function of the Self, which intervenes at crucial junctures of life if one is open to it.

A series of extroverted activities, including traveling alone followed by her decision not to marry at the first opportunity, could be something she had to do to deal with the restless animus. She became more independent and confident in dealing with practical difficulties alone. Yet, in spite of all her self-earned independence, she managed to remain unidentified with her professional life and was open to what fate brought in terms of marriage and motherhood. Her reaction to motherhood was an interesting combination of her natural inclinations, fear, and a feminine receptivity. Her grateful acknowledgement of her husband's positive influence on her emotional life reflects a well-balanced relationship to her animus and its outer projection.

It is, however, not possible to speculate why some women, like this one, manage to develop in cooperation and companionship with their archetypes better than others. The openness to life's "accidents" and a conscious assessment of the events at different points help certain people to shift and change like a river that finds new channels after natural impediments. Fate, in these cases, is invited to help the conscious personality whose capacity is after all limited.

ENDNOTES

32 Harding, Esther (1933), *The Way of All Women*, New York: Longmans, Green & Co.

33 Erikson, Erik (1964) "Inner and Outer Space - Reflections on Womanhood" in *Daudalus*. Spring, pp. 582 - 606.

34 Guggenbuhl-Craig, Adolf (1977) *Marriage Dead or Alive* (Tr. by Murray Stein), Zurich, Switzerland: Spring Pub.

35 Hillman, James (1975) "Betrayal" in *Loose Ends*, Zurich: Spring Publication, pp. 63 - 81.

36 In this regard see Manisha Roy's *Bengali Women* (which went to second edition in 1992). The practice of finding a religious guide - a guru -even among young married women continues especially among the urban middle-class Hindu women in India. How much of this practice is to answer to the sincere spiritual needs or how much is just to follow the custom for family honor, is hard to tell.

37 Wolff, Toni (1956) "Structural Forms of the Feminine Psyche" (Tr. by Paul Watzlawik), Zurich: C.G. Jung Institute - Private Printing.

CHAPTER 5

Aging Years
and Death

In the last chapter I tried to describe the relationship of an adult woman to her archetypes as they find expressions through her socially available roles and choices. Let us look at the last years of a woman's life when the natural biological process of aging may create new problems. Some of these problems begin to manifest as the middle years of life arrive and may continue to accompany her till death. She usually suffers from a number of psychosomatic symptoms characterized by anxiety, depression, hypochondria, even addiction. In medicine, a whole group of such symptoms are categorized under "senile difficulties." The psychological component to such symptoms have a lot to do with the fear of death and aging, both of which have increasingly reduced emotional support from the advanced and so-called progressive and modern societies today.

Typically, in a woman's life around the age of 50 and above, when she moves from the stage of a reproductive female to a menopausal one, the psychological and physiological implications are serious, although neglected in most cultures. As in puberty, she faces a drastic change in her body and her metabolic system, often accompanied by severe hormonal disruptions. Again, like the time when as a girl she faced the menstrual trauma, her surroundings help her little, if at all, in coping with this transition. Today, she has access to various hormonal treatments to mitigate her physical discomfort from menopause. However, some of these treatments are highly controversial, but her society and culture offer almost no help for her to realize the transformative value of this archetypal suffering that is repeated in every woman's life. In a monograph titled *Change of Life: A Psychological Study of Dreams and the Menopause* (1984), Ann Mankowitz discusses the possible reasons of this neglected crisis. Her observation that the absence of a rite of passage for this critical transition in a woman's life may be due to the short lifespan of women in all cultures until this century sounds quite plausible.

The argument that this indifference resulted from patriarchal bias that ignored post-fertile women does not necessarily apply to many old and tribal societies. These societies helped both men and women to age, if not gracefully, at least to nurture some hope for special status deserving respect from the society. They became custodians of tradition and special skills. A number of respectable and specially endowed positions were reserved for the aged. Both men and women could become storytellers, healers, shamans, and spiritual leaders. In this way, they could be useful and creative force in their societies and cultures. In her book *Male and Female*, the well-known anthropologist Margaret Mead, from her many years of work with primitive cultures observes:

> The post-menopausal woman and the virgin girl work together at ceremonies from which women of childbearing age debarred. (page 180)

And:

> In many primitive societies girls before puberty and women after the menopause are treated very much as men. A society that has not defined women as primarily designed to bear children has far less difficulty in letting down taboos or social barriers. It is very significant that the Mundugumor, even though they have an institutional framework based on the exclusion of women from initiation into the men's cult, both repudiate women's childbearing functions and let women into the mysteries of the sacred flutes.[38] (page 229)

In rural India, a woman in her advanced age looks forward to her power as a matron whose motherhood now is extended to a sociological one. She is a mother not only to her family, but to her neighborhood or even her community, her village. Women, children, and even men sometimes, come to her for advice, help, and nurture. She may help in delivering babies, an art she has learned from many of her own pregnancies. Or she may shift smoothly from her motherhood to her role as a grandmother and become an indulgent grandmother who withdraws from the position of power more and more, and tells stories and teaches customs and rituals to younger women and treat young grandsons as special beings to be spoilt. Whenever there is a birth, wedding, death, or any other special event marking a transition, she may be consulted to tell exactly what needs to be done. Details for such rituals are important to propitiate the right god or goddess, and she becomes the custodian of the cultural mysteries that are sacred because they deal with the supernatural world. In this way, her decreasing involvement with her personal family and greater interest in her community and impersonal aspects of life, such as social work or politics and religion, indicate a new development. More and more educated middle-aged women are running for political offices. Social roles and customs help her to go through this phase. A woman who remains overly engrossed in her family or fails to go along with these changes may attract considerable social criticism. As a result, she suffers alienation and loneliness.

A somewhat similar situation prevailed in the West until the last century. In several European countries, there were women who guarded folk customs and legends. In countries such as Ireland and England, there are still old women in remote villages who remember and tell tales and stories through winter nights. There were old women who were approached for white and black magic to cure various physical and mental ailments. A significant change, not only in the style and standard of living but also in the demographic picture during the last hundred years, has taken place in the West and to some extent all over the world.

New Longevity, New Challenge

The life expectancy of women is even more marked than that of men due to an enormous improvement in the medical care in childbirth and through effective birth-control measures. Women today live much longer than in previous times and can increase the span of their old age and non-reproductive phase significantly by controlling pregnancy and being health-conscious. According to *Woman's Body: An Owner's Manual* (1978) by Diagram Group, life expectancy for the average American woman in 1978 was 76 years compared with 50 years around the turn of the century. About one-third of her life thus falls in the non-reproductive, postmenopausal phase. Therefore, many women attain the so-called middle age long before their menopause. This choice has several significant implications as far as a woman's psychic life is concerned. She can be relieved of the engrossing childbearing and rearing activities sooner than her female ancestors and this newfound energy must find outlets for expression.

This situation is an outcome of advanced medical technology along with the raised awareness among women that they have a choice of shortening the period to be devoted to motherhood. The free time left to her in her advanced years is not always as promising as the choice before it. Is she, with the help of her newfound consciousness, more capable of channeling her energy in creative and productive activities? Her animus in this respect is again vital in helping her go through this period without stagnation or over-activity. It is often observed that a middle-aged woman in America or Western Europe becomes overactive and takes up many kinds of responsibilities, some to her benefit and some not.

It seems to me that the animus at this stage of her life may have to help a modern woman to step back and reconnect to her feminine self, something from which she may have been estranged. Depending on the kind of life a woman has led so far, the help of the animus would be essential either to take her to a collective community life (as in the case of an Indian mother) or to take her back to a feminine world, if a woman has spent most of her adult life in a profession in a masculine world.

The following dream of a 61-year-old professional woman portrays this point almost comically:

> I hear soft music coming from the woods. It could be a flute or a guitar, not clear. I follow the music to find the player. I've a feeling that it's a handsome young man, and as I look for him, my heart and soul fill with a pleasant emotion. After searching for a while, I see through the trees a young man, as I guessed. I go close and then notice that he is really wearing women's clothes. He turns toward me and smiles, and now I see how feminine he really looks. I wonder if he's a transvestite. I feel a strong emotional connection to him without much repulsion, although he is wearing long earrings and even nail polish on his fingernails.

Psychological Implications: Letting Go and Developing Impersonal Interests

The return to the feminine world with the help of the animus also prepares a woman for a further stage of introversion leading toward death, of which the anxiety is paramount in modern people. Although with the help of modern medicine and the higher standard of living we have succeeded in controlling birth considerably, we can only delay death, not control it. Since our power to control birth gives us the illusion of a superior power over nature, we are baffled about how to deal with this threatening inevitability of death, the end of our physical existence.

It is possible to surmise that, since now our old age is longer than before, this period of time may be necessary to unwind from a highly engrossing material involvement in our modern life. C.G. Jung, in his paper "The Stages of Life," elaborates on the possible importance of even further introversion of an aged person today to compensate for his long, extroverted materialistic life.[39] In fact, it is no exaggeration to say that Jung's whole psychological philosophy and practice are primarily devoted to work after the first part of life. A woman who has sacrificed a part of her instinctive life for the sake of consciousness and her psychological development must reconnect with her basic life, and here the animus helps her as a guide to return to her feminine roots. In real life, it's expressed through good judgment, good perception, the right kind of action with determination, all qualities of an ego that has established an intimate relationship with her positive animus.

The tendency today is to attack the problem of aging and death through an extroverted approach to solve it as efficiently and expediently as any other problem. Many hospitals and medical institutions now have separate geriatric departments, dealing with how to help aging patients cope with such an undesirable event. Such a social-work attitude may deprive the natural evolution of an aging woman or man toward a solitude that is necessary before death. Irene de Castillejo, in her book *Knowing Woman*, stresses this point:

Many old men and women are cheated in their essential solitude, and kept continually focused on outer things by the mistaken kindness of the young and their own unawareness of their need to be alone. We die alone. It is well to become accustomed to being alone before that moment comes.[40]

The author is advocating an atmosphere where an aged person can find her solitude to come to terms with her life, perhaps to allow the projections to withdraw and to move inward to assimilate her archetypal traits further. Loosening the bonds of her personal relationships, she may discover another kind of relationship that goes beyond personal love and possession. She now finds an emotional link to the archetypal world where peace – rather than hopes, desires and power – reigns. Her physical existence with all its trappings that ego has worked hard to achieve is now subordinate to the Self. Again, her animus helps her to realize that her ego is only a minuscule part of the eternal and indestructible Self, and thus the physical death is, after all, no great loss. She can be and can remain part of the eternal scheme forever.

Following the scheme I used before to see the relationship between the woman and her archetypes, it can be said that at this stage, the withdrawal of her projections of her contrasexual and other unconscious aspects must take place before she is ready to accept death. A touching and disturbing yet common example to the contrary is portrayed by the novelist D.H. Lawrence in his classic book *Sons and Lovers*, when he describes the last days of the mother of his autobiographical hero, Paul.

Paul's mother, who has projected all her Eros and ambitions of an unfulfilled life onto her son, has bound him to herself in an inextricably strong tie, which has smothered both with bittersweet love. She cannot die or prepare for death because of her unresolved projection of her erotic animus onto her son. Neither she nor her son can be free to help her over the threshold that will bring transformation to both. Lawrence describes this deadlock thus:

> Then she pretended to be better, chattered to him gaily, made a great fuss over some scraps of news. For they had both come to the condition when they had to make much of the trifles, lest they should give into the big thing, and their human independence would go smash...She thought of the pain, of the morphine, of the next day; hardly ever of the death. That was coming, she knew. She had to submit to it. But she would never entreat it or make friends with it. Blind with her face shut hard and blind, she was pushed towards the door. The days passed, the weeks, the months.[41]

This situation, penetratingly described by the masterful novelist for many pages, perhaps points to the psychological fact of a woman's inability to introvert and withdraw from the outer world of her personal possessions and projections. Her animus projection stays with the object stubbornly. The ego hasn't let go of her attachment to her son gradually to make room and condition for the projection to withdraw naturally. As a result the animus is stuck with her son and is not free to live inside herself and be her own spiritual guide to her death. Occasionally, we meet people who have lived, albeit unconsciously but naturally, allowing themselves and their archetypes to move from projection to projection leading toward a transcendence.

Some of the physiological changes and behavior that occur at this stage of life are interesting to note. After menopause, the change in hormonal balance in a woman's body may be manifested in masculine characteristics. One often encounters married couples in their 60s or 70s or even 80s, where a stout, heavy-set, deep-voiced wife is followed by a soft-skinned, timid-looking, shrunken husband. This physical reverse, although connected to hormonal changes, may also correspond to the psychological overlap between the woman and her contrasexual archetype. An interesting example of this is recorded by Vieda Skultans in the article "The Symbolic Significance of Menstruation and the Menopause" (*Skultans*,1970) wherein rural Welsh women described such transformation as "Women turn into men inside."[42]

These changes in both physical and psychological characteristics may indicate that a woman's sexual identity is not so important anymore. She need not belong to the feminine branch of the human biological group. She can easily overlap with the male members of her species. The opposition between her conscious ego and her contrasexual archetype has created tension throughout her life, pushing her into action and experience; and now the battle, struggle, and confrontation of that creative tension are finally over. She is still a woman who is reconnecting with her feminine principle, an archetype that is beyond sexual connotation. It is a spiritual existence that is beyond the sexual, and only by going through sexual identity could she achieve this goal. She must now go back to Nature, the source of all life and death, all differences and variations.

This aspect of overlap and merging of sexual identity is similar to the overlap and mingling between the conscious and the unconscious worlds of senile experience. For example, an old woman dozes off while telling a story and, after a few minutes of traveling into the sleep world, softly comes back to the conscious world and again picks up the thread of the story she was telling. The boundary between the conscious and the unconscious worlds (like the boundary between life and death) has become vague, and an old woman or man who can slide between the waking and sleeping states so easily may also be prepared for crossing the threshold of death relatively easily.

Animus as Spiritual Guide to Death and Beyond

No matter how difficult and demanding aging is in the life of a modern woman, she can also gain a last opportunity for a creative growth toward a peaceful renunciation of the world. For this a heroic effort is needed to go beyond the stereotypical image of the menopausal, aging, and therefore worthless woman. Already pioneers have ventured into the area to set examples for their sisters. In her monograph mentioned earlier, Ann Mankowitz describes such a woman who could overcome her frustrations and despair by learning to keep close contact with her unconscious.[43] In an ongoing process of analysis guided by a woman analyst, this woman could benefit from the symbolic message of her dreams, which come from the depth of the unconscious. She could reconnect with her archetypal roots and heal herself to move on to a renewed identity and fuller life. When a society does not offer a healing renewal through ritual initiation at this critical juncture of a woman's life, she must do it within herself with the help of her own archetypal links.

No other time is as critical for a woman today as the post-menopausal last phase of her life because menopause not only ushers her to her old age, she also loses all that which gave meaning to her as a woman so far. Emphasis on sexual attractiveness and capacity to bear children are two important stereotypic boosting her society and culture provide to enhance her self-image. Now with the loss of these abilities she must find a new identity. Again, her animus can be helpful in this last part of her search for a new identity that does not depend on the socially supported stereotypes but rather on the deeply felt self-knowledge that is acquired by a painful reckoning with oneself.

The value of the contrasexual archetype in this last phase of her life leading to her Self, her ultimate and core existence, is depicted in mythological and religious symbols such as Orpheus and Krishna. These hero-gods have used their lyres or flutes in luring mortals irresistibly to an emotional ecstasy equal to paradise. Emma Jung, in her essay "Animus and Anima," describes this phenomenon well by going into the power of music as part of the luring and magical guidance of the animus.

She writes:

> In this sense, music is spirit, spirit leading into obscure distances beyond the reach of consciousness; ... music admits us to the depths where spirit and nature are still one – or have again become one. For this reason, music constitutes one of the most important and primordial forms in which woman ever experiences spirit. Hence also the important part which music and the dance play as means of expression for women. (Emma Jung, 1974, page 36.)

And again:

> An important function of the higher, that is, the personal animus, is that as a true psychopompos, it initiates and accompanies the soul's transformation. (Emma Jung, 1974, page 33.)

This spiritual aspect of the animus mediates between the woman's conscious ego and the unconscious while it is also one of the personifications of the latter. Besides offering the woman the capacity and power of reflection, differentiation, and self-knowledge, the animus also helps a woman to be connected to the spiritual problems of her time. She can become a vessel and a guide for a group of individuals. This spiritual connection that may be dormant in her earlier years (except in such cases as Joan of Arc) comes to a culminating point in her later life before her death. The time now comes when she must free herself from all identifications and projections and stand vis-à-vis the transpersonal spirit. By differentiating both her feminine and masculine archetypes, she not only helps her archetypes to develop, to humanize and be free to mingle with the transpersonal again but is also available to the next generation. This is a woman's contribution to her gender and to humanity. Without her body and her life of action, creativity, and relationships from birth to death, archetypes are unable to find living expressions. In outer life, until this stage is achieved by a woman to free herself from all her projections, she is helped by the figure of a spiritual teacher, a priest, a guru, or a guide to carry this projection of her guiding animus.

Most religions throughout history have offered such a figure, which only recently has been replaced to a great extent by the personage of an analyst or a therapist. In a world where the changes of time and mood also make drastic changes in religion, such new trends may be inevitable. The practice of psychoanalysis and psychotherapy, beginning with Sigmund Freud over a century ago, is gaining ground in its increasing variety and proliferation of practice among educated people. The value of the analytical framework for an individual woman or man to realize the workings of the inner life is increasingly significant because we live more and more in a milieu of rational consciousness only to be marked by occasional outbursts of the unconscious tendencies in the expression of negative archetypes because of their banishment from the conscious ego. With the help of an analyst or therapist, a woman can realize her projections of both poles of the archetypes and other aspects of the unconscious, which are foundations of the external behaviors and feelings.

Among all the problems of life, aging and death are the most critical ones, and a woman (or man) can cope with this existential crisis with some equanimity only when she knows and feels connected to something beyond the finite biological life. Since she had to sacrifice her old beliefs in a supernatural world to gain a consciousness, the only choice left to her now is to make a conscious alliance to the archetypal world, which is eternal as well as healing.

ENDNOTES

38 Mead Margaret (1969) *Male and Female*, New York: Dell Publication

39 Jung, C. G (1933) "The Stages of Life" In *Structure and Dynamics of the Psyche* Collected Works, vol 8, paragraphs 749 - 795.

40 De Castillego, Irene Clarenmont (1972) *Knowing Woman: A Feminine Psychology*, New York: Harper & Row, page 162

41 Lawrence, D. H (1913, 1948)) *Sons and Lovers*, London: Penguin Books, pp. 467 - 468.

42 Skultans, Vieda (1970) "The Symbolic Significance of Menstruation and Menopause" In *Empathy and Healing: Essays in Medical and Narrative Anthropology*, ed. Vieda Skultans, pp.639 - 651.

43 Mankowitz, Ann (1984) *Change of Life: A psychological Study od Dreams and the Menopause*, Toronto: Inner City Books.

CHAPTER 6

Concluding
Remarks

Approaching the end of this book, I realize that it has been only a first attempt to come close to the mysterious workings of the archetypes in the changing life of a modern woman and her culture.

I tried to show that enduring social institutions and customs reflect deeper archetypal needs of the collective psyche. Institutions change only when the archetypes themselves must find newer forms of expression. From this viewpoint, institutional changes, for better or for worse, reflect the eternal need for inner change and vice versa. A good example is the archetype of mothering. While the introduction of contraceptives has changed the present-day mothering style in the sense of rational choice in control of birth of children, the archaic emotions remain strong. Many women still become pregnant "accidentally," and many women behave like devouring and killing mothers despite all the sophistication and idealization of a modern version of motherhood. The cases of child abuse may not be just direct expressions of frustrations of parents or parental figures like teachers and priests. More and more women in analysis are confessing their inexplicable and embarrassing need to harm their children not only in fantasy.[44] The eternal need for archetypes to be realized in both positive and negative poles is very much visible in all directions today. Social roles and institutions which are not adequate for a balanced expression of both poles will eventually change. That, too, is archetypal.

Closely related to this point is the variation of forms in social and cultural systems for the expression of the same archetypal needs. I tried to demonstrate this point by using examples from two very different civilizations in the first part of the book. These variations are important to remember also in the case of women of different socio-economic strata even within the same society and also different stages in the life of the same woman. In other words, how similar needs are recognized and lived or repressed depends a great deal on the social, cultural, and personality backgrounds of the individuals. As values must change at different stages of life, so do needs that shift in intensity, depending on one's age and circumstances. Apart from such issues of relativity in the cultural and other influences on a woman's psychology, there is one other important theoretical goal I set out to achieve.

C.G. Jung's concept of the contrasexual archetype, the animus, has been under criticism in recent times not only among non-Jungians but also some feminist Jungians themselves, especially in America.[45] This has much to do with the change in time and place as well. Jung's own observations came from his time and culture of the first half of the 20th century. Despite his capacity for a fair amount of objectivity and visionary intuition, noticeable changes have taken place in economic, social, and psychological life in the West, and especially in America since his lifetime. The serious and enthusiastic search for a new feminine identity in the last 50 years in America, England, France, and Germany was not yet visible in Switzerland before Jung's death or even a decade afterward.

Psychological concepts, like any other, must undergo revision in view of newer experience. The objection to the animus as being the masculine side of a woman has to do with a confusion regarding masculinity and femininity right now. Some who see "masculine" simply as a sexist term want to do away with the whole idea of masculinity as part of a woman's psyche. Others object to Jung's listing of certain qualities as being feminine and masculine. If Eros, for instance, seemed more a feminine trait in Jung's experience, we need not stick to his experience when we discuss his theories and can easily shift according to our own experience and observations when we discuss our time.

Right now, all definitions of masculinity or femininity are unclear and, therefore, flexible. The justification for using these terms to indicate certain opposed styles of being grounded in two different sexes is in its invaluable symbolic meaning. Masculinity is not only what men in a society are supposed to be but also a certain mode and atmosphere that underlie a masculine approach psychologically and symbolically. Since the human psyche moves much slower than outer forms and ideas, there is always a lag. Besides, as long as the two sexes remain different biologically, the difference in psychology must follow, albeit with changes and overlaps. If the feminist argument against acknowledging unconscious elements of masculinity in a woman comes from the anger and rejection of the male world and male dominance, it is understandable, but is not a valid enough argument to reject the theory.

I personally find the concept of animus very useful despite its changing images and expressions (as described in this book) because it explains certain tendencies and experiences in a woman that cannot be explained otherwise. To determine that my views were not entirely personal, I conducted a survey among 40 Jungian analysts and 15 non-Jungians who were slightly familiar with the concept. Only two out of these 55 people, both men and women, saw no need for such a concept to describe feminine psychology. Most of them felt that a concept such as this helps to differentiate the complexities of the psychology of a woman in this changing time. How else can we name feelings and actions that are not our own, yet originate inside us and look very much like what our brothers or husbands or male colleagues might do naturally. They also agreed on the animated emotion created by some identifications and projections. It's also difficult to explain strong emotions associated with many deram images and verbal utterances inside dreams evoking feelings of awe and power the only term for which can be 'numinous.' The power of a strong attraction to many things "masculine" and somewhat unknown somewhere inside women must come from something deeper in the unconscious.

I find the concept of the contrasexual archetype useful in understanding not only the individual woman's psychology but also in assessing the collective atmosphere of modern time, which is psychologically more "masculine" than "feminine," as defined in the beginning of this book. As a reaction to this predominantly masculine world, a swing back to the feminine pole is already visible. The crying need for a new identity of today's women and the vague reaction to all this by men, along with ever-mounting problems in politics, education, religion, and personal relationships, perhaps indicate a need for a much larger and deeper change than that of a few women becoming conscious of their condition.

Even women themselves who had to develop more masculine values and attitudes to survive and to adapt, are now rebelling against such one-sidedness. Conversely, those women who remained "feminine" and offered the opposite viewpoint to the masculine mode are now also rebelling against such meaningless and wasteful sacrifice.

C.G. Jung was a pioneer, introducing a psychology that could be termed more feminine than masculine, because of his urgent plea for recognition of the irrational, paradoxical, and dark aspects of our lives and psyches. He also attracted our attention to the existence of psychic realities such as archetypes, which also need to change forms as time changes. I have tried to point out, throughout this book, how archetypes such as animus must also change in its images and connotations as their human carriers and their cultures change. Gods, heroes, and leaders all changed during last century, sometimes beyond recognition judged by old definitions. Speaking of heroes, Saint George and Odysseus were two out of many Western heroes who symbolize the attainment of consciousness by killing the dragon or annihilating the negative aspect of the feminine archetype. They not only killed the dragons but also became strong and mature by going through the dangerous challenges posed by the bewitching and disabling temptations of the feminine archetype. Today, the struggle of the heroes has shifted considerably. The challenge now is to relate to the dangerous anima, not just to kill or conquer her. A man or woman today is weak and incomplete if he or she does not incorporate the dark femininity within as well as recognizing and befriending the personal shadows. Before that is possible, individual men and women must learn to understand and accept the nature of these archetypes and their workings in their lives. This is another reason to refine our theoretical tools as much as possible so that they help us to better understand our life's irrational and sometimes chaotic experiences.

A Schematic Theme of the Interplay of the Ego and the Archetypes in a Woman's Life

In the second part of the book, I tried to capture the experiential aspect of the feminine and masculine archetypes in the ongoing life of individual women in America. At this point, I would like to suggest a structural scheme that underlies the interplay of the ego and the archetype of the animus in a woman's life from birth to death. A similar scheme can be suggested for a man's life as well. Like all theoretical schemes, this is only an ideal, hopefully helping us to make some sense out of chaotic events of life. This scheme also suggests that the archetypal development of a woman's personality corresponds to her sexual and biological maturation, despite the lack in our knowledge of the real connection between the physical and psychic levels at this time. The basic assumption behind this structural scheme is that human instincts founded on archetypes seem to strives for a balance between different parts of psyche. In a woman's development, her feminine archetype and her animus need to balance each other either in conscious actions or in the unconscious through compensations. Working toward a conscious balance seems important; otherwise, the repressed elements may erupt in compensatory activities that may be disruptive such as psychosomatic illness and neurotic symptoms. Immediately after birth and immediately before death, the identity of a woman remains asexual and androgynous. Some societies recognize this aspect by giving names to the child that are neuter or dressing it in unisex clothes. However, the identity begins to establish itself, perhaps even before this socially recognized period, by the mother's unconscious attitude toward a male or female child. Psychologically, her femininity begins to establish itself by the time she is dressed as a girl and is referred to as a girl by others. She also lives within the feminine group of nurturing and caring women, almost totally, until the time when she is exposed to her father or other male family members. This custom, however, is changing rapidly in America and some parts of the world, where fathers are taking a strong part in bringing up a child even from infancy. At any rate, it seems to me that her contrasexual archetype is consciously activated in her after she is already a girl in others' eyes. Following this, her whole life goes through a series of alternate phases of identifications with her own archetype and the animus in many roles and actions. Most of this happens not only through identifications but also projections, especially in case of the realization of the contrasexual. The feminine phases are also characterized by a period of introversion, while the animus phases are more extroverted. If her familial and social roles do not help her to live these phases alternately, either of the archetypes may remain unconscious, only to be compensated for later. Since no woman's life runs this ideal course, there are always maladaptations and problems, some of which may amount to serious ones.

In fact, it is possible to argue that an imbalance may encourage the woman to compensate in a creative way unless she remains stuck in a phase generating neurosis, which, in turn, may be the compensation itself. This balance between the two archetypes is necessary not only along the life cycle but also at different contexts in everyday life in today's complex world.

Following is a simple diagram showing the approximate ages of the woman's life, alternating the conscious identification of feminine and contrasexual archetypes along with an introverted and an extroverted phase, respectively. When she is acting out the one, the other is in the unconscious waiting for the expression in the next phase. My division of these phases by seven years is somewhat arbitrary but is what I often observed in people's lives. By no means is it definitive. As mentioned above, sometimes in today's complex world a woman may have to shift between the two archetypal personas within even a single day.

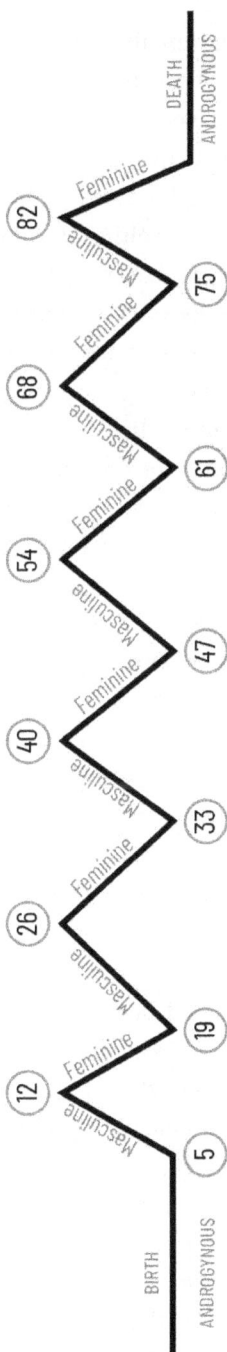

While the above scheme remains speculative based on clinical observations and life experience, it can be used as a yardstick to determine the points of neurotic development in a woman's life. It can also help us to have an overview of a woman's life process and discern the outline of her personality. In the life stories described in this book, it is possible to see that some of the problems came either from unlived or over identification with the animus. Others lacked adequate feminine identifications.

This is only one way to look at the interplay between a woman and her archetypes. The advantage of this scheme is that it gives a concrete dimension through life's biological scale since most of our roles are determined by ages and stages of life.

As I came to the last phase of a woman's life, I found myself going beyond the pressing issue of the identity crisis. Archetypes in this stage of life contribute to the transformative activity of the woman's psyche. This is the time when she integrates more than projects. All her projections are gradually withdrawn, and she comes to an end of the play of life to await death, the end of her biological existence. The animus that helped her enrich her personality and bring resolution to the conflicts between her yang and yin, or the animus and the femininity, can guide her now to serve her Self, the mysterious transpersonal aspect of our personal psyche, which dictates and acts quietly and subtly throughout our lives. She transcends her sexual identity and is eager to be reunited with the great Mother because she is the child of Nature. The archetypal contents that help an individual with creativity, intensity of emotions, and meaning, are also responsible for their own transformation from the instinct to the spirit beyond, but only through human life. The birth of a new spirit seems to take place before physical death. Beyond every death linking the individual to eternity, the archetypes continue, only to be re-lived in another individual's life within the context of a family, society, and culture.

Thus, archetypes can give us a secure identity by helping us understand our intangible connection to the mysterious depth of the collective unconscious. In this godless world, now, more than ever, we need such a connection to something larger than life, something that transcends our mundane and overly materialistic existence.

ENDNOTES

44   I had a vivid example in my practice of the force of archetypal need that had to express itself through an immoral action. A mother of 56 had an uncontrollable urge to push her son over the balcony railing of an eight-floor balcony. She came to analysis because she was afraid that she must be losing her mind to have such a feeling to kill her only son whom she adored. After several months of analysis it was obvious that she strived to be the 'best' mother who never had any grudge against her son or against herself as a perfect mother. The negative pole of the archetype had to surface literally with a vengeance.

45   One of the early publications in this respect is Naomi Goldenberg's "A Feminist Critique of Jung" In Sign: Journal of Women in Culture and Society, 1976, vol.2 pp. 443 - 449. This trend seemed to have somewhat changed in last half a century due to an ever emerging complexity in sexual and gender identitites including sex change operations following years of painful sufferings in some cases. Although the percentage of such cases remains small at this moment, the linguistic innovations (LGBTQ) indicate a definite recognition of such alternative sexual orientations if not in mainstream American culture at least in the liberal realms of politics and mass media.

ADDITIONAL REFERENCES

Arditti, Rita et.al. (1984)*Test-Tube Woman: What Future of Motherhood?* London: Pandora.

Barz, Helmut (1991) *For men Too: A Graceful Critique of Feminism,* Wilmette: Chiron.

Binswanger, Hilde (1963) "Positive Aspects of the Animus." Spring, 82-101

Bruno Battelheim (1962) *Dialogues with Mothers,* New York: Avon Publishers of Bard, Camelot, Discus and Equinox Books.

De Beuvoir, Simone (1949) *The Second Sex,* New York: Knopf.

Dunn, Nell (1965) *Talking to Women,* New York : Ballantine Books.

Edinger, Edward F. (1972) *Ego and the Archetype,* New York: Putnam

Francella, Fay and Kay Frost (1977) *On Being A Woman: A Review of Research in How Women See Themselves,* London, New York: Tavistok Publications.

Grinnell, Robert (1973) *Alchemy in a Modern Woman,* Zurich: Spring.

Gimbutas, Maria (1982) *The Goddesses and Gods of Old Europe,* Berkeley: Univ. of California Press.

Handerson, Joseph (1984) *Cultural Attitudes in Psychological Perspective,* Toronto: Inner City Books.

Hannah, Barbara (1953) "Animus Figures in Literature and in Modern Life" Lecture given at the C.G. Jung Institute, Zurich, Switzerland.

Harding, Esther (1975) *The Way of All Women,* New York, Harper Colophon.

Hillman, James (1985) *Anima: An Anatomy of a Personal Notion,* Dallas: Spring.

Johnson, Robert A. (1990) *Femininity Lost and Regained,* New York: Harper & Row.

Jung, C. G. "Anima and Animus," *Collected Works,* vol. 7, pp 188-211

------------"Instinct and the Unconscious," *Collected Works,* vol. 8.

------------"On the Nature of the Psyche," *Collected Works,* vol. 8.

------------ "The Syzygy: Anima and Animus," and "The Self", *Collected Works,* vol. 9,11

------------"Marriage as a Psychological Relationship," *Collected Works,* vol. 17.

Lederer, Wolfgang (1968) *The Fear of Women: An inquiry into the enigma of Woman and why men through the ages have both loved and dreaded her,* New York: Harcourt Brace Jovanovich Inc.

Luke, Helen M. (1985) "The Life of the Spirit in Women." in *Woman, Earth and Spirit: The Feminine in Synbols and Myth*, New York : Cross Road.

Matoon, Mary et all (1989) "Is Animus Obsolete?" in Shirley Nicholson(ed.)*The Goddess Re-Awakening*, Wheaton: Quest/ Theosophical.

Moore, Robert & Douglas Gillette (1990) *King Warrior Magician Lover: Rediscovering the Archetype of the Mature Masculine*, San Francisco: Harper

Murdock, Maureen (1990) *The heroine's Journey: Woman's Quest for Wholeness*, Boston & Shaftesbury: Shambhala.

McLaughlin, Kathleen(1985) "The Unemployed Animus: The Curse of the Unlived Life." *Anima*, vol. 11/2,

McNeely, Anne D.(1991) *Animus Aeternus: Exploring the Inner Masculine*, Toronto: Inner City Books.

Mumford, Lewis (1961) *The City in History*, New York: Harcourt Brace.

Neumann, Erich (1954) *The Origins and History of Consciousness*, Princeton: Princeton Univ. Press.

Orbach, Susie and Luise Eichenbaum (1984) *What Do Women Want?* Glasgow: Fontana/Collins.

Rowland, Susan (2002) *Jung: A Feminist Revision*, Malden, MA : Blackwell Pub.

Roy, Manisha (1982) *The Animus, Women And Cultures* (Diploma Thesis), Zurich: C.G. Jung Institut-Zurich.

----------------(2015) *My Four Homes: A Memoir*, Asheville: Chiron Pub.

Rubin, Lillian B. (1979) *Women of a Certain Age: The Midlife Search for Self*, New York: Harper & Row.

Salmon, Sherry (1986) "The Horned God: Masculine Dynamics of Power and Soul" in *Quadrat*, vol.19, No. 2, Fall.

Sanford, John A. (1980) *The Invisible Partners: How the Male and Female in Each of Us Affects Our Relationships*, New York: Paulist Press.

Sharpe, Sue (1976) *Just Like a Girl: How Girls Learn to be Women*, London / New York: Penguin Books.

Singer, Milton (1972) *When a Tradition Modernizes: An Anthropological Approach to Indian Civilization*, New York: Praeger.

Stein, Robert (2001) *Love, Sex and Marriage*, Woodstock, CT: Spring publication.

Steven, Anthony (1982) *Archetype: A Natural History of the Self*, London: Routledge & Kegan Paul.

von Franz, Marie Louise (1978) "Shadow, Anima and Animus in Fairy Tales" *Interpretation of Fairytales,* Dallas: Spring.

Wehr, Demeris (1987) *Jung and Feminism: Liberating Archetypes,* Boston: Beacon Press.

Wolff, Toni (1956) "Structural Forms of the Feminine Psyche," Tr. by Paul Watzlawik, Zurich: C.G. Jung Institute Private Printing.

Young-Eisendrath, Polly and F. Wiedemann (1987) *Female Authority: Exploring Women Through Psychotherapy,* New York: The Guilford Press.

DESCRIPTIONS OF TERMS AND CONCEPTS AS THEY ARE USED IN THIS BOOK

ARCHETYPES are universal images or ideas which come from the collective unconscious. Abstract by themselves, their effect can be realized only through emotional experiences which are influenced by the individual's subjective response. The archetypes are based upon forms from existing cultural symbols.

In turn, they influence our behavior and emotions. Archetypes have personal and transpersonal, as well as an individual and a collective, dimensions . When experienced, archetypes can generate ambivalent and strong emotions including numinosity giving a transcendental quality. Yet, archetypes are transformed through human experience within social and cultural roles while, in turn, transforming the human beings in the process. If the outer roles and customs are cut off from the archetypal source, they become stereotypes without intensity and meaningful vitality.

Archetypes reside in the depth of the psyche of humanity, in general, which C.G. Jung termed, the **COLLECTIVE UNCONSCIOUS.** In dreams, fantasies or psychoses, images which have nothing to do with personal life-experience emerge from the collective unconscious. Such images and the emotional experience associated with them can also emerge at critical points of life. Religion, mythology, folklore and all forms of artistic creation are often symbolic representations of archetypes from the collective unconscious which is the greatest source of creativity and healing, as well as destructive powers.

A COMPLEX is an emotionally-charged group of ideas and images which always has an archetype at the center. This archetype is closely connected to associations and emotions derived from personal experience. Something in the environment (a word, a smell, a person, etc.) can activate a complex with strong emotions that may disturb normal functioning. When we speak of Mother Complex, we mean that there are gamut of autonomously-charged emotions behind the actual relationship with the mother, and she may have only very little to do with the triggering mechanism. So, complexes are autonomous and have a tendency to move by themselves unless the person is conscious of it.

CONSTELLATION means a mysterious activation of a set of emotions associated with a core complex. When it is said that something is constellated, this means that the emotional reaction to a situation is not obvious or understood.

EXTROVERSION is the outward movement of psychic energy or subjective interest to an object. An extrovert thinks, feels and acts in relation to the object. **AN INTROVERT,** on the other hand, thinks, feels and acts toward the subject. Subjective consideration is of primary importance and the object is secondary. Introverted energy is important to bring balance to the very extroverted lifestyle today. Creativity needs both kind of energy to conceive and to express. Families and society often impose extroversion or introversion through value judgments while educating children. These attitudes make a big difference in one's approach to life problems . What an extrovert must do may be devalued by the introvert, and the former may never appreciate the agony of the latter. These attitudes are significant elements of one's personality.

INTUITION is the irrational psychic trait which acts through the unconscious and can perceive more than what is visible in the immediate reality. That is why intuitions are called "flashes" or "insights" which are hard to substantiate by data available to observation. Intuition is often the only door to the unconscious. Intuitive understanding combines facts with intuitive insights.

EGO is the center of the field of consciousness and is related to the outer reality through a consciousness of continuity and identity. Ego is the conscious part of the total personality, which includes both conscious and the unconscious elements. Ego is shaped and conditioned strongly by one's social and cultural environment, and can gain strength only when related to the unconscious and when subordinated to Self, the center of the total psyche.

SELF is the regulating center of the personality and is transpersonal. It represents the totality of one's personality including the conscious and the unconscious parts. Like all archetypes, Self is a priori and is related to wholeness and is represented in all the symbols of totality, wholeness and healing such as the ultimate divinity. Self is, also, the innate potentiality for one's need to be oneself, a unique identity each person must realize in life. Its organizing and healing capacity is discernible in critical moments of life when, either through dreams or through outer events, Self sends a message to change the course of life. Ego often has no choice but to follow such dictations.

SHADOW refers to those attributes, either positive or negative, which are unknown to a person, and is that part of the personality which is nonadaptive to the conscious world at the time and are denied and repressed. If repressed long, shadow elements can be quite autonomous and can take over the ego. For example, when a priest suddenly becomes a criminal, he is being controlled by his worst shadow . In occupations and professions, we sometimes choose our shadows to work with because unconsciously we are attracted and fascinated by our unlived shadows and our psyches appear to have a need to integrate at least parts of them. Integration, or assimilation of parts of shadow, can release extra psychic energy, but, it is one of the hardest inner works in life. Therefore, we often use outside situations, people and things to carry our shadow projections before we can recognize that these qualities actually belong to our own unconscious personalities.

PROJECTION, IDENTIFICATION AND INTEGRATION are discussed in details in the Introduction of Part II of this book.

Psychologically, every man and woman is endowed with bisexual characteristics as they are also biologically endowed with both male and female hormones. C.G. Jung used the terms **ANIMA** and **ANIMUS** to refer to the personifications of the elements of the collective unconscious as they are experienced by the two sexes . In other words, they refer to the unconscious feminine side of a man's personality and the unconscious masculine side of a woman's personality, respectively. Anima and animus are contrasexual archetypes which ideally should function as bridges to the collective unconscious. For example, a woman is helped by her animus to remain connected to her unconscious. She usually experiences different aspects of her animus through projections on outer men, objects, ideas which represent masculinity. Male dream figures which have strong emotional impact on the dreamer are personifications of the contrasexual archetype, the animus . Conversely, feminine figures in a man's dreams and fantasies represent the various elements of his anima.

The development of a woman's animus depends on many factors. Her personal father, cultural images of masculinity and her psychological constitution are vital factors. If a woman is brought up without a father figure, her mother's animus would substitute this figure unconsciously. When the animus is undeveloped and not related to a woman's ego, she may be identified with it in both positive and negative aspects, but more negatively because of the lack of integration through consciousness. She, then picks up the stereotypic opinions and fads of masculine ideas from the prevailing culture and time. Such identification can alienate her from her feminine identity instead of helping her to remain connect ed to her unconscious archetypes.

Since the cultural images and ideas of masculinity and femininity may change over time, the traits that characterize either the personal animus or the collective ideas of masculinity also change. Psychologists, more than others, must remain flexible to adapt to such changes; otherwise, we remain stuck in age-old stereotypes about what a woman is or what masculinity is— something which used to be fashionable one or two generations ago. The difficult question that then arises is: does man and woman own some kind of innate masculinity and femininity that are endowed bio-sexually? Answer to such a question must wait until we have more knowledge and understanding about the biological, genetic and psychological makeup of men and women. At present, we need to reify and differentiate, as much as possible, the psychological and cultural factors so that certain levels are kept in mind.

In this book, the terms animus and masculinity within a woman are used interchangeably sometimes. A clarification of how these terms are used may help the readers to understand the author's viewpoint. The term, masculinity, is used here more to connote the style of being naturally pertaining to man as opposed to the feminine style of being naturally pertaining to woman. This style of being is instinctive (biological), psychological and socio-historical.

It is now well known from many anthropological studies that most cultures encourage the expression of physical aggressiveness among male children more than among their female counterparts of 2 to 2 ½ years of age. Whether expressions of physical aggression is a necessary adaptive tool or not, it seems to be strongly associated with the later development of ambition and drives in most men. In most cultures, men are socialized to be more self-reliant and competitive for outer achievements such as jobs, studies and social recognitions. In keeping with these expectations, men, also learn to be more abstract in thinking, developing organizational skills, dealing with ideas more than with things and people. The male sexual organ in itself is synonymous to the kind of aggressiveness mentioned here. Hilde Binswanger, the analytical psychologist (1975), explains how the sexual and reproductive encounter between a man and a woman shows different modes. While the man penetrates the woman, she receives only one sperm out of millions for fertilization to take place. The woman's power of selectivity then moves further into her need to wait quietly for the long gestation period when creativity takes place in the darkness of the womb, and no further encounter between the sperm and the egg is possible. By nature, therefore, Binswanger concludes, man's aggression is balanced and faced by woman's receptivity, selective choice and quiet creativity.

Whether we can stretch this bio-sexual analogy to male and female psychology fully is hard to determine. However, one can evaluate such observations with intuitions, feelings and emotional experience. While exceptions are many, trends may be seen among men and women which support the above analogies.

This recent trend in not only changing sex-roles but, also, admitted needs in developing the feminine aspects among men, and may very well be a need for balance to a one-sided masculinity during the last several generations . Young fathers are demonstrating open affection and nurturance toward the children, and young mothers often earn the salary allowing their husbands to take care of the households. Men seem to be increasingly aware of the development of their Anima.

FEMININITY is used throughout this book as the style of being that comes naturally to a woman. This style is a combination of biological or instinctive drives and other socially-learned and culturally-adaptive behaviors. Her needs to build a nest, to mate and to mother go hand-in-hand with her needs to do and be things that men have been associated with for generations . What has been defined as masculine by her culture and society has been repressed inside her, and today, she is determined to live it because she has been devalued as a woman who never learned to be as capable as men. This revolution has its psychological component. She must develop her animus, and not just be identified with it or be controlled by it. Therefore, what is feminine as defined by today's American culture is a bit confused, albeit including the old habits of being dependent and passive partners of men . However, for the sake of her identity, a woman has to know and feel what makes her comfortable and self-assured as a woman although she may be confused at times. Despite the changing definition of femininity, her identity as a woman comes from her biological and sexual being as well as what her society and culture define to be feminine. If the latter is changing, she is still a woman bio-sexually, and she knows what is expected of her before she can see the changes around her.

Therefore, both these terms have biological, sexual, psychological and symbolic meanings and connotations specific to men and women at a given time, society and culture.

ABOUT THE AUTHOR

Manisha Roy, PhD, IAAP, is a trained geographer and anthropologist and received her diploma in analytical psychology from the C.G. Jung Institute of Zurich, Switzerland in 1982. She has been in private practice in Cambridge, Massachusetts and is a training analyst and in the faculty of the Jung Institute of Boston for 30 years. She has taught both anthropology and analytical psychology at several universities including Universities of Colorado, Denver, Long Beach, California and the University of Zurich, Switzerland. Dr. Roy has lectured all over the world. Among numerous publications she has 32 articles and 10 books, including My Four Homes, published by Chiron Publications, in Asheville, North Carolina.

Dr. Roy lives in Cambridge, Massachusetts with her husband, who is a retired physician and author.

www.ingramcontent.com/pod-product-compliance
Lightning Source LLC
Chambersburg PA
CBHW020611270326
41927CB00005B/288